MAKING

SPACE GROW

Barbara Taylor Bradford

SIMON AND SCHUSTER • NEW YORK

Published by Simon and Schuster
A Division of Gulf & Western Corporation
Simon & Schuster Building
Rockefeller Center
1230 Avenue of the Americas
New York, New York 10020

Designed by Eve Metz
Manufactured in the United States of America

1   2   3   4   5   6   7   8   9   10

Library of Congress Cataloging in Publication Data

Bradford, Barbara Taylor, date.
     Making space grow.

       1. Interior decoration.   2. Room layout (Dwellings)
I. Title.
NK2113.B7   747'.8'83   78-10767

ISBN 0-671-22473-5

TO LEIF PEDERSEN

ACKNOWLEDGMENTS

My grateful thanks to Pauline V. Delli Carpini for her assistance with research and her tireless hunting down of appropriate illustrations; Leif B. Pedersen and Joan Blutter for access to their design files; Gleb Derujinsky for special photography; and the following designers whose work stimulated so many of the ideas and discussions in this book: Milo Baughman; Eugene David Bell; Eileen Bickel; Louisa Cowan; Abbey Darer; Angelo Donghia; John Elmo; Charlotte Finn; Virginia Frankel; Carl Fuchs; Ginny Gray; Gayle Grimm; Jerome Hanauer; Albert Herbert; Nina Lee; Emy Leeser; Nancy Maggard; Derek Mason; Tai and Rosita Missoni; Giorgio Morabito; Edmund Motyka; Virginia Perlo; David Poisal; Shirley Regendahl; Annie Lawrie Ryerson; Douglas Sackfield; Michael Sherman; Janet Shiff; Robert C. Simon; Joyce Vagasy; Jane Victor; Peggy Walker and Frances Wise.

CONTENTS

INTRODUCTION, 9

1 . EXPAND SPACE BY VISUAL ILLUSION, 13

2 . MAKE LARGER USE OF SMALL ROOMS, 35

3 . CREATE A ROOM WITHIN A ROOM, 50

4 . DECORATE SPACE FOR TWO CHILDREN, 73

5 . SPACE STRETCHERS FOR ONE-ROOM APARTMENTS, 84

6 . HOW TO SHAPE LARGE SPACE, 104

7 . CLEVER STORAGE IDEAS, 122

8 . RECOVERING WASTED SPACE, 139

INTRODUCTION

Space is a precious commodity today and nowhere is it more precious than in the home. Very few people have enough space to adequately suit all of their living needs, yet with skyrocketing rents and the increasing cost of building and buying, most people are literally making do with the space they have, rather than moving into larger homes.

Consequently, almost everyone finds himself faced with numerous space problems. Often these problems seem insurmountable, especially for the inexperienced home decorator.

For example, I know from the mail I receive from readers that varying kinds of space problems are a common denominator in all types of homes across the country. These problems can be very upsetting because most people want to get the utmost in comfort, function and style in their homes.

The most common problems readers write to me about are: insufficient number of rooms, especially prevalent in a growing family; rooms that are too small to function properly; rooms that have to be shared by two children; and rooms that have to serve more than one purpose.

Singles and newlyweds who occupy studios or one-room apartments are confronted with the problem of how to stretch space so that it functions well for all living needs. On the other hand there are an infinite number of problems with large rooms, where space has to be shaped and controlled to work efficiently.

Also, the inefficient use of storage or the lack of it is a major headache in most homes, whatever their size. Very few of us have enough space for storing all our necessary household items.

Yet all of these seemingly insurmountable problems can be solved through expert planning and imaginative decorating ideas that help to make space grow. Well-planned space not only makes a room function successfully on all levels, it makes the occupants feel comfortable and at ease.

MAKING SPACE GROW

3 areas of activity

The basic challenge is to know your specific needs and to organize space to meet those needs—for family activities, entertaining, relaxing and working. Whether a home has a little space or a lot, it is possible to shape and control that space without moving any walls or making any structural changes.

You can expand space through the use of dual-purpose furniture, skillful furniture arrangements, furniture designed specifically to save space, color schemes and materials that expand space by visual illusion—to name only a few ways. There are an infinite number of design and decorating techniques that can be used for exciting and creative effects, as well as for functionability. With a little guidance, knowledge of decorating and self-confidence, almost anyone can decorate in his own style to produce an environment that is efficient, comfortable and high in good looks.

It was the brilliant architect and furniture designer Mies van der Rohe who so aptly said: "Less is more." And this dictum was his design philosophy throughout his life. In essence, it was the most prevailing and dominating factor in everything he designed—skyscrapers, rooms, even a simple chair. He believed that any room would look and live with more style, graciousness and comfort if it were sparsely furnished with the minimum of essential pieces that were fine of line, utterly functional and handsome without being ornate. All of his rooms, whatever their size, were spacious and light. How right he was and how applicable his ideas are today, living as we do in the era of the space squeeze.

We might also consider the Japanese and take inspiration from their solutions of space problems over the centuries. Their homes have airiness, lightness, a clean and open look. This ambience is created through the elimination of all unnecessary objects which produce a cluttered effect, and through the use of sleek wood floors often covered with unobtrusive flat mats, shoji screens used not only at the windows but to divide and demarcate space, and low furniture that is perfectly scaled to fit limited space.

The Japanese in general treat space in such a way that it produces a flowing, expansive look that is tranquil and therefore soothing. And this is a vital consideration today. Everyone wants to live in an environment that satisfies inner and aesthetic needs, as well as day-to-day living requirements. In fact, a home is more important than it ever was, since it is the ultimate retreat and haven away from the pressures of our hectic working schedules.

Creating an environment that is ideally suited to you and your family can be relatively easy, if you know what you want and have some basic decorating guidelines at your fingertips. You can then design a home that gives you pleasure and comfort, that reflects you and your tastes, even when space is at a premium.

Point of departure

This book was designed and written to help you do this. It shows you how to make space grow and function for the ultimate in convenience and attractiveness. There are clever and imaginative decorating and design solutions for almost all the common space problems you are likely to encounter, whether you live in an apartment or a house, and whatever its size.

All of them are by well-known interior designers, who through their expertise, experience and talent know exactly how to conquer space and make a room live up to its potential. Many are designed for small or medium budgets, all are easy to modify to suit your specific needs.

1·EXPAND SPACE BY VISUAL ILLUSION

Any room, whatever its size, can be made to appear much larger than it really is through the use of visual illusion. While this does not actually increase the amount of physical space, it does make the room *look* more spacious so that it is less confining, and is more comfortable and attractive.

There are many different ways to create this visual illusion. It can be done with colors that recede and therefore appear to push walls out; it can be created with certain materials with a reflective quality, such as mirrors, metallic wallcoverings, metal tiles and sheets of polished copper. When applied to the walls, all of these materials suggest added depth. Wallcoverings with a three-dimensional pattern, murals with a trompe l'oeil effect and supergraphics also create the illusion of depth and dimension, which makes a room seem larger than it is.

Apart from all the materials and colors you can utilize on the walls and ceiling, there is a wide range of floor coverings that help to make the room seem that much larger.

For example, any pale or light-colored floor covering is ideal for stretching space underfoot, whether this is unpatterned wall-to-wall carpet, vinyl tiles, sheet vinyl, ceramic tiles, marble, or wood painted in white or pale colors. Natural wood floors which have been highly polished and left bare also expand the floor area considerably.

Various types of furniture help to add airiness within the room and so promote a more spacious ambience, again through optical illusion. Glass, steel-and-glass, chrome-and-glass, brass-and-glass and Plexiglas or Lucite pieces—all have a floating, almost weightless quality and therefore appear to take up less space. This is because see-through materials don't stop the eye, as do woods, especially dark wood or dark lacquer finishes. So, if there is more to see, you feel as though there is more space and openness.

Furniture that is painted white or a pale tone, wicker and bamboo pieces and furniture that has a light or airy scale also help to give a room a lighter look.

13

MAKING SPACE GROW

This medium-sized room appears to be tripled in size and will function much larger than it really is, all through clever illusory effects. The abundant use of white gives the entire room a light, airy, expansive feeling that is both restful and refreshing. The white walls and draperies open up space, while the luxurious fake-fur rug brightens and stretches the floor by optical illusion. To emphasize the spacious ambience, a minimum of furniture was used. Each piece was chosen for its lightness of scale or its see-through qualities. The bamboo chair and ottoman and the Lucite coffee table take up little space visually, while the white-upholstered sofa blends into the background. The shelf slab, which appears to float on the main wall, is a splendid alternative to a console table, since it takes up no floor space. In combination with the eye-catching silver graphic, this shelf creates a focal point in the room. The slender modern clock adds balance and echoes the natural coloration of the bamboo pieces. The white tubs for the plants and white lamps reiterate the one-color theme, with the plants themselves adding just the right amount of accent color. Sparse use of accessories and general lack of clutter further the clean, open look. Nubby fabric on the sofa, fluffy rug, bamboo and Lucite combine to create an interesting textural play in the room. Designed by Giorgio Morabito, A.S.I.D.

14

Certain fabrics can be used in schemes where illusion is the decorative premise. For instance, voiles, muslins, organdy, cottons, Belgian linens, smooth silks and satins promote a sense of airiness, because of their lighter weight. Especially effective are fabrics that are unpatterned in white or pale solid colors, and fabrics that have a very small or open pattern, such as trellises or light plaids. Stripes and ticking produce a feeling of height and are ideal to use in small rooms with low ceilings. Wallcoverings similarly patterned tend to push walls out, and by opening up an area a feeling of more space is achieved.

Several window treatments help to carry through this theme. Tailored window shades, vertical blinds, shoji screens, sliding panels, shutters, and panel tracks holding fabric are particularly good because they introduce crisp, neat looks and don't visually intrude into the room or produce an overpowering effect. Simple floor-length draperies with French headings, full-length sheers or casements will blend into the background. Because they don't stop the eye with strong contrasts, they too will emphasize spaciousness.

When some or all of the elements just mentioned are brought together in a room, the effects they create can be exciting, imaginative, often dramatic, and they will expand space through the simple trick of fooling the eye!

When you understand a few illusory tricks you will be able to handle them skillfully to create the special ambience you are seeking. And incidentally, don't forget that when you expand space by visual illusion you are saved the bother and expense of making structural changes.

INGENIOUS WAYS TO PUSH WALLS OUT

Walls form the largest expanse of unbroken space in any room. So they should be your first consideration when you make your decorating plans. When walls have been effectively treated to a few visual tricks they do the most to broaden the horizons of any room. They add width, length and depth, and can sometimes stretch space endlessly for a feeling of infinity.

Don't forget the ceiling when you formulate your decorating scheme, since this too is a large area of unbroken space. A variety of different materials can be utilized to make it seem higher for an airier look, especially worth considering when you are decorating a low-ceilinged room or when you simply want to suggest more height.

The materials you select for your walls or for any decorating project depend on three things: personal taste, the decorative look you prefer, and the amount of money you can afford to spend.

15

Innovative decorating by designer Peggy Walker gives a tiny "high-rise" dining area a greater look of spaciousness, which adds considerably to the comfort and good looks of the space. Her tricks: broad strips of mirror run floor-to-ceiling across the back wall, lots of pale cream on the walls and floor, and an understated but effective window treatment composed of shantung shade-cloth vertical blinds. The strips of mirror were inexpensive and simple to put up. They reflect the vertical blinds' subtle linear look and create a three-dimensional background of gentle optical illusion. The translucent shades fit within the window frame for a smooth, tailored effect; both filter glare and let in light when closed or frame the view when open. The round rosewood table and chairs play curvaceous complement to this interesting straight-lined look, and the mirrored theme is even carried through in the table setting. Circular mirrors set in painted red squares make unusual placemats for tableware and the centerpiece. The glass-and-pewter chandelier casts up-and-down lighting that illuminates the area effectively. A plant was the only other addition, since the designer did not want to create a cluttered look in the small dining spot.

16

Certain patterns help to push walls out and so open up a room through optical illusion. Trellis patterns are especially effective as illustrated in this charming converted porch. Designer Shirley Regendahl selected a lime green-and-white trellised wallpaper, peppered extravagantly with yellow and tangerine flowers to achieve the desired effect. The narrow room immediately took on a sense of width and airiness. To camouflage the slanting roof, the pattern was continued over the ceiling in beamlike strips; broader panels were painted white to give it more height. Since the room was particularly narrow, the designer selected white-painted-and-glass furniture that has a light, almost weightless appearance. For this reason it does not intrude visually on limited floor space. Twin étagères float up the wall, further promoting the feeling of height, yet because of their color and lightness of scale, they blend beautifully into the background. See-through glass shelves add to the overall airy look of the furniture, as does the glass top on the circular table. All the pieces of furniture are of bamboo-turned aluminum enameled white. Curving loveseat provides seating for three, yet again takes up little space because of its shape. The designer utilized a smart decorating trick at the windows. The three French doors were treated to bright tangerine window shades, and because this vivid color advances into the room, walls surrounding the window appear to recede even more in contrast and by optical illusion.

[handwritten note:] Wess advance in Contrast to wall receding

Sometimes it is possible to create a greater feeling of spaciousness by giving up a little floor space. For example, this handsome living room takes on totally new dimensions through the addition of an arched wall built in front of three small windows at one end of the room. It is a brilliant idea that introduces a feeling of added space because the eye is led out and beyond. The illusion is one of endless garden vistas both inside and out. Plywood paneling that matches the paneling on the other walls was utilized to create a false wall, set two feet away from the windows to create a garden area. The plywood paneling that features natural knots and burls of real wood is easy to handle yourself, and the arched wall design can be adapted to any wall size and window arrangement. It can also be utilized in any room where there is a need to suggest spaciousness with illusory tricks. The arched entrances, topped by roll-down bamboo shades, also promote a sense of extra height and introduce architectural interest. The combination of glass and white wall beyond appears to recede and in effect push the end wall out by illusion. Glass shelves hung in the windows contain small plants, interspersed with pottery pieces. The floor area accommodates larger plants. Fluorescent ceiling lights on the garden side of the arched wall provide artificial sunlight when needed.

18

Obviously certain materials are cheaper than others and will be more suitable if you're working on a limited budget. Paint and certain fabrics and wallcoverings are all relatively inexpensive. On the other hand, mirror and metal tiles, mirror panels, polished copper panels and custom-designed fabrics and wallcoverings are more costly.

You must also consider the cost of the labor involved, and undertstand that certain materials are more intricate and complicated than others. Naturally, if you are handy with a paint or paste brush and a staple gun, you can cover the walls with a fabric or wallcovering yourself, and paint them even more easily. But mirror and metal are not so easy to put up, and in most instances these materials may have to be handled by a professional, who will know how to do the job properly. This is particularly important when mirrors are involved, as they can easily shatter if not treated with great care.

Economics

Only you yourself know what your personal taste really is, and so you should be guided by your preferences. Select materials for the walls that please you the most. However, it is important to remember that if you have a family, the materials chosen should be compatible with their tastes also. There is nothing worse or more upsetting than decorating a room that other people feel uncomfortable or ill at ease in, so do keep in mind your family's taste before you settle on materials.

The materials talked about earlier all create individual decorative effects; which one you select depends on the overall mood you wish to introduce.

MIRRORS

One or more mirrored walls can produce a shimmering, cool and reflective look that is highly effective in expanding by illusion. Mirror used in this manner is very glamorous, also somewhat sophisticated since it connotes high style. So don't choose mirror if you are planning to use Early American or rustic furniture. These combinations are simply decoratively out of kilter, and you won't like the finished result. Antiques, reproductions, traditional and modern furniture all blend beautifully with mirrored walls, and you will be pleased with the sparkling results. Dramatic effects can be achieved when glass-and-steel, Plexiglas or Lucite furniture is utilized in a mirrored room. When mirror reflects shiny or see-through materials, space appears to stretch out into infinity.

Current fad

An important point to remember is that when only one wall is covered with mirror it must reflect decorative objects or furniture. When mirrored panels or tiles face an opposite wall that is blank, a great deal of its decora-

Must reflect objects

19

Interior designer Jane Victor, A.S.I.D., broadened the horizons of a small living room through a little brilliant decorating. To push out the main wall and widen the room optically, she lined the middle section with mirror, running it floor to ceiling. This was balanced by two armoires which protrude into the room slightly and create an alcove effect. In contrast with the armoires, the mirrored section is more effective since it visually recedes even further. The designer selected French antique furniture that is small in scale and upholstered it in pale fabrics to underscore the intrinsic lightness of the pieces. A traditional steel-and-glass table virtually floats in the center of the room because of its see-through qualities. A pale-colored area rug stretches floor space and controls the seating arrangement for a truly compact look. As the room needed a focal point, the designer turned the mirrored wall into a center of interest, adding slender antique marble pedestals and plants for extra decorative interest. The mirrored wall reflects the piano in the far corner, as well as the small seating arrangement for interesting double images. Color scheme is apple and beige.

20

EXPAND SPACE BY VISUAL ILLUSION

Designer Emy Leeser totally changed the dimensions of a small, boxlike room and introduced a feeling of space and soaring height through visual illusion. Her technique was the skillful positioning of large-sized murals. The murals come printed on straight wallpaper panels, but the designer angled them across two walls to create this space-stretching effect. The murals are in red, purple, maroon and white on a dark eggshell background. By carrying the mural at left across the corner and onto the adjoining wall, the room actually takes on a circular shape. This is further underscored by the circular loveseat and chair, all upholstered in bright red on "birdcage" bases of polished steel. The tables have the same "birdcage" appearance, and because of their airy quality seem to take up little space visually. For color coordination in the room, the designer used an area rug flashed with the same tones in the murals. In a room where unusual shapes make a strong statement, two interesting white modern lamps help to fulfill the look.

tive potential is lost, the room will look bare and sterile. Of course, the mirror will push out the wall upon which it is used, but the overall effects won't be quite as interesting or eye-catching.

Apart from introducing illusory space expansion in living rooms, dining rooms and bedrooms, mirrored walls also work miracles in bathrooms and halls, especially those that are truly confined. Mirror works well in any room where space is at a premium. It pushes walls out, creates depth and interesting decorative effects because of the double images it produces, and of course it reflects general overall light and bounces it back into the room for an airier look.

Ceilings

Interior designer Jane Victor suggests carrying mirror onto the ceilings of bathrooms and halls for fabulous space expansion. Since these rooms are not general living areas the totally mirrored space does not become irritating or overpowering.

There are many decorative mirrors to choose from that will further the feeling of depth with a highly personal effect. Another of Ms. Victor's visual tricks is to hang crystal or metal wall sconces or candelabra holding candles on a mirrored wall, because reflections of light against mirror produce shimmering good looks.

WALLCOVERINGS

If you cannot afford to use mirror, or if this decorative look does not appeal to you, consider some of the other reflective materials which are less expensive. You won't get quite the same exciting effects as mirror creates, but you will introduce a feeling of expanded space because they do help to make walls recede and reflect light to a degree.

This is particularly true of metallic wallcoverings with silver or gold backgrounds. They are available in all price ranges today and in an incredible number of patterns. Some of these are plain, others are overpatterned with another color for a dimensional feeling. These wallcoverings can be used with all types of furniture, provided the pattern itself is compatible with the style of the furniture. For example, with period furniture you should use a traditional pattern, with modern furniture you should select one that has a contemporary design. Plain metallic wallcoverings go with both.

A metallic wallcovering can be used on only one wall, all the walls, and even be taken up onto the ceiling. It depends entirely on your personal taste and the decorative overtones you want to introduce.

Angelo Donghia, one of the most brilliant young designers in America today, uses plain metallic paper on the ceiling in two rooms of his New York duplex apartment. In his beautiful green-and-white living room, fir-green

22

Many kitchens suffer from lack of space, and because of equipment and storage items it is difficult to stretch space in any other way than by visual illusion. Interior designer Charlotte Finn, A.S.I.D., was faced with a tightly knit combination of stove, sink, dishwasher, counterspace and refrigerator in an extremely confined space. Her solution was to coat the entire kitchen with a white-and-silver geometric wallcovering which reflects light and gives it a whole new, airy feeling. She cleverly took the wallcovering onto all the cabinet doors and the ceiling as well as the walls, and in so doing created smooth, flowing space since the eye is not stopped by any contrasting colors. Adding to the optical effect of expansiveness is the wide white translucent window shade which spans all three windows, joining them for a smooth, unbroken expanse of space. The shade is trimmed with red braid to match the red countertops, the only accent color in the room. The floor was covered with white vinyl tiles to stretch space underfoot.

walls are juxtaposed against a ceiling covered entirely with unpatterned silver paper. This serves to raise the ceiling, reflect light and create soft color and textural play. In his elegant banker's gray bedroom the ceiling is lined with plain gold paper for the same reasons. Around the molding and baseboard in this room are strips of silver lamé fabric that add extra sparkle against the gray walls.

Incidentally, the entrance and second floor hallways of Angelo's duplex are lined entirely with mirror to expand space, but also because the designer believes that mirrors provide a feeling of glamour and infinity, and also make a neutral background for the inclusion of accessories, especially plants and flowers.

23

This narrow family room is actually a converted basement. A long blank wall presented decorating problems. To give the room dimension and to broaden its horizons, it was divided into two distinct areas. A portion of it was lined with floor-to-ceiling bookshelves, which immediately added much-needed architectural overtones and depth. The adjoining area was covered with two wall murals which have a trompe l'oeil, hand-painted look of windows and views. They appear to push the walls out, and lead the eye out for a real three-dimensional effect. The two "window" murals offer a vista of the French Riviera in a stunning mingling of blue, green and brick tones. The vinyl murals are printed on straight panels and are pre-pasted, pre-trimmed and strippable, making them easy to put up. To emphasize the rustic mood, ceiling beams were added in this area. Apart from visually expanding the feeling of space by seemingly making the walls recede, the murals introduce a "windowed" look in a basement without windows. The murals are ideal to use in small dining rooms or in any room that needs expansion by visual illusion.

Metallic wallcoverings can be used with other reflective materials for unique looks. For example, if you cannot afford to use mirror throughout a room, you could cover one wall with it and the others with a silver or gold metallic paper. Or you might consider teaming metallic papers with high-gloss lacquer paints, utilizing the two on alternate walls. The combinations are endless.

Metallic wallcoverings work in every room of the home, but they are ideal for small kitchens and bathrooms. Today these wallcoverings are specially treated to withstand moisture and staining, so of course they are naturals for these two rooms. Since many are pre-pasted, pre-trimmed and strippable, they are simple to put up yourself.

Metal panels and tiles are other reflective materials that help to expand space by optical illusion. Polished copper panels and chrome tiles are especially effective and can be used in most rooms. Metal materials covering all the walls tend to create a harsh look and soon become tiring with constant viewing. So it is best to put these on only one wall in frequently used living areas, for the most successful results. Copper tiles or panels tend to introduce a warmer, more rustic look; chrome tiles a strictly contemporary feeling. They are effective in kitchens and bathrooms for introducing these different moods. Metallic tiles are extremely practical because they wear well, are easy to keep clean and, because of special finishes, don't tarnish.

Wallcoverings with a mural design or a trompe l'oeil effect are excellent materials for opening up a room. This is because the designs tend to lead the eye out and beyond and produce great depth and add a three-dimensional quality. They are available in various price ranges and some of the inexpensive ones are equally as effective as the ones custom-designed.

In this skillfully designed dining room by Frances Wise, three elements come together to counteract lack of space. The designer used lots of white, an unusual wall mural, and lightly scaled furniture to produce stunning good looks in very limited space. The white wall-to-wall carpet, white walls and draperies expand the room, while the colorful mural adds a three-dimensional effect on the back wall. The mural is printed on a plain white background and comes in individual panels. The designer used four panels to cover the wall and took the plain white companion wallcovering onto the other walls in the room. Acrylic-coated, the mural and companion wallcovering are pre-trimmed, pre-pasted and washable, and are easy to put up yourself. The scaled-down chrome-and-glass dining table and chrome-framed yellow chairs have a light, floating look, as do the other pieces in the room. They help to continue the airy mood created in the room.

MAKING SPACE GROW

These wallcoverings can be put on all the walls or on only one, depending on the look you prefer. Most come with a plain companion wallcovering that can be carried around the room for coordination, should you decide to use a scenic, mural or trompe l'oeil on only one wall.

These designs are marvelous space expanders for small, dark or windowless rooms because of the three-dimensional quality they invoke. Also, they introduce a view in a room without one. Consider using them in kitchens, bathrooms and entrances.

Supergraphics, geometric dimensional wallcoverings, and those with open patterns such as trellises and plaids, make walls recede for an airier look. Some produce a feeling of greater height in a room, others can actually change spacial dimensions by optical illusion. They too can splash across one wall, or on all the walls, and even be carried up onto the ceiling.

OTHER WALLCOVERING IDEAS

Interior designer Angelo Donghia recommends the use of sheets throughout a room to further the feeling of space by illusion. In fact, decorating with sheets has become one of his trademarks. His own designs for a leading manufacturer of bed and bath linens are highly decorative, and he has created many schemes built around sheets. He considers sheets to be the cheapest and most decorative fabrics available today, and they are simple to handle for the novice decorator.

Angelo's technique is to use matching sheets throughout an entire room for a coordinated look and a sense of flowing, unbroken space. When one pattern is repeated everywhere the eye is not stopped by contrasts. He staples sheets onto the walls, sometimes tents the ceiling, and then repeats the same sheets for upholstery and draperies as well as on the bed. The finished results can be pretty and feminine or tailored and crisp, depending on the patterns and colors used. Incidentally, sheets are extremely practical; they can be removed and laundered easily, retaining their fresh look. Most of the new fiber combinations require no ironing, another asset.

That good old standby, paint, is probably the cheapest product to use on the walls of a room. Certain colors and finishes are better than others for expanding space by visual illusion. For example, all pale colors recede and appear to push walls out, and they also reflect light and bounce it back into the room. Good space-expanding colors are white, pale yellow, pale blue, pale green and light cream. These tones are even more effective when they are repeated throughout a room in a monochromatic scheme.

Glossy lacquer finishes introduce reflective overtones and so help to expand by optical illusion. Even dark lacquers tend to do this, although these

This small foyer was dark and cluttered and seemed more confined than it really was because of poor decorating. Designer Shirley Regendahl gave it a sparkling new face and expanded its actual space through clever choice of materials and colors. She opened up the walls, previously painted dark red, by covering them with a light-as-air, bamboo-patterned vinyl in white with yellow leaves. For real coordination and to blend numerous doors into the background (only one shown here), she used the wallcovering as decorative inserts and painted the surrounds bright yellow to match floor and ceiling molding. The designer also painted the ceiling in a paler tone of yellow to push it up and introduce more height. She created an interesting custom look with sleek vinyl asbestos tiles, which simulates an area rug without interrupting flow of space. Green, yellow and orange tiles were put down to form the rug effect, the central orange tiles repeated on the periphery for color coordination. The campaign chest provides storage and surface space in a compact, neat manner. Mirror, plants and small accessories were added for a finishing touch, to create a foyer which appears to be twice its real size.

are most successful when utilized on only one wall. Pale-colored paints and those with a lacquer finish work well with all the materials mentioned earlier in this chapter, and these combinations are worth considering if you are working on a limited budget.

FLOOR PRODUCTS THAT STRETCH SPACE

To successfully expand space by visual illusion it is vital to include the floor in your overall decorating scheme. When a floor is not correctly treated it can counteract the illusory effects you have created on the walls.

All solid-color, unpatterned floor coverings tend to stretch space un-

27

derfoot, because they produce an unbroken look which does not distract the eye. These include wall-to-wall carpet, plain wood floors, vinyl—whether it is sheet or tile, ceramic tiles, asbestos tiles, linoleum, marble, and painted wood floors.

Those materials which have a highly polished or shiny finish create an even better effect, because they help to reflect light within the room.

All pale colors are ideal because they make any floor area seem much larger. However, certain darker tones can be effective, especially the patent vinyls, marble and polished wood floors, This is particularly so when they are against pale walls and ceilings.

Although plain floors produce a great sense of unbroken space, it is not necessary to dismiss a patterned floor covering entirely, if this is your personal preference. Certain patterns can create a feeling of extra space by optical illusion because they lead the eye out, suggesting width and length. Among these are some geometrics, large, open patterns such as plaids and basket weaves, diagonal-striped effects in a large scale, large checkerboard designs and windowpane patterns.

However, each one must be considered carefully before you make a final choice; you must bear in mind any other patterns you have used elsewhere in the room, such as for upholstery or for draperies. Be certain the floor pattern is going to blend well and not fight the others, creating a busy, overpowering look.

Painted floors have become very popular in recent years and stunning looks can be created, whether the floors are painted one solid color or treated to an attractive stenciled design. For the best effect, a floor should be painted white, cream or any other pale color. Several coats of paint are necessary to produce a handsome look. The floor must then be finished with a few coats of clear polyurethane varnish or shellacked to seal and protect it. If you are stenciling a design onto the floor, this must be done after the paint has dried and before you add the varnish finish. Interior designers such as Leif Pedersen, Jane Victor, Nancy Maggard and Janet Shiff favor these floors and insist they are extremely hard-wearing and easy to maintain. They work well in most general living areas and can be very pretty in children's rooms.

Jane Victor sometimes utilizes vinyl in custom designs to create dimensional effects on a floor which help to expand space optically. She began one floor in a child's room with a large red vinyl square. This was surrounded by four wide strips of white vinyl, the white edged by four strips of red, and on and on for a graduated effect until the floor was entirely covered.

Angelo Donghia favors dark patent-finish vinyls, such as navy, black and brown, either plain or interlaced with diagonal stripes, for space expansion underfoot. But he always balances these dark, mirror-like floors with pale walls for a floating, open look above the dark tones.

28

A pretty mélange of pastel parfait colors was mixed together to create a feeling of lighthearted, summery airiness in this nursery designed by Nancy Maggard. The floor was painted white and stenciled with bouquets derived from the print used throughout the room. Apart from its decorative effects, the stenciling expands and uplifts the floor and becomes a charming background for the furniture. This includes pieces of old-fashioned wicker furniture and an antique crib turned into a loveseat. They were painted white to promote the airy mood of the room and enlivened with a lovely floral chintz, color-keyed to the entire scheme. Pale orange-sherbet walls and white-painted woodwork recede and in combination with the floor open up the area considerably. The designer utilized a light-looking treatment at the two windows, to make them appear taller than they really are. The treatment is composed of pouffed and bowed draperies of the chintz, backed up by pink-and-white striped window shades. In spite of its delicate appearance, the nursery is highly practical. The window shades are functional room darkeners for naps and early bedtimes, and they wipe clean with ease. So do the pieces of furniture; while the floor by Gayle Grimm was shellacked to a high gloss to retain its good looks and wear well through hard treatment.

FURNITURE THAT CREATES AN AIRY MOOD

Furniture takes up the most space in any room, but it's impossible to do without it. You can select furniture that does not overly intrude on floor space, or which appears to take up little visual space.

All furniture made of see-through materials is perfect for expanding space by optical illusion. Glass in combination with chrome, steel or brass is the most obvious choice, as well as items made of Plexiglas and Lucite. Some pale-toned or white plastic pieces are also effective. As I mentioned earlier, see-through materials do not stop the eye, as does dark wood, and because you see through and beyond the furniture there is a sense of lightness within the room.

The majority of furniture made of these see-through materials is modern in design, although a few traditional pieces are available. Naturally all of them are perfect in contemporary settings, but some pieces can also be used in a room where period furniture makes the definitive statement. This is because the see-through materials do not compete with the wood tones of the traditional pieces and actually seem to disappear into the background.

Wood furniture that is painted white or a pale tone immediately takes on an airier feeling, and so seems to disappear into the background. If walls are painted a pale color or white, the light-colored furniture will blend and disappear even more. Many interior designers are now using the technique of lacquering the frames of antique or reproduction pieces white, to help promote this fresher and airier look. White frames in combination with soft or light-colored fabrics, or other upholstery materials, are most effective.

Wicker furniture, once relegated to the garden or terrace, now takes its place indoors with great ease. Because of its light look, it too can expand the spacial effects in a room, and it can be used in any general living area. Apart from this, it produces a charming summer feeling all year 'round; one which is lighthearted and cheerful. Wicker looks and lives best when it is painted white or left in its natural state. Bamboo and cane are similar in feeling to wicker; they too can stretch space visually.

The scale of each piece of furniture is important and it must be of the right proportions for the size of the room. Obviously, finely scaled furniture introduces the greatest illusion of space, whatever the size of the room. Heavy furniture produces an overpowering, crowded look, especially if it is made of dark wood, and it should be avoided at all cost.

Always pay attention to upholstery materials whether it be fabric, leather, suede, or manmade products. Plain materials are usually better to use than patterned ones, and of course pale and light colors do much to add lightness to any piece of furniture.

Chocolate brown, masses of white, reflective materials and airy furniture help this sitting room area of a bedroom to expand. The white predominates, showing up in the plush nylon carpet, the draperies, window shade, painted furniture and lampshades. It is thrown into high relief by contrasting chocolate walls treated to lacquer paint for a glossy sheen. The large floor-to-ceiling mirror, which covers the central section of the main wall, actually gains additional sparkle through the use of a Lucite dressing table placed flush to it, and Lucite lamps. This clever arrangement produces an infinity of images and pushes the wall out for dimensional effects. The white-painted furniture is light in scale and airy in feeling, and arranged in front of the mirrored wall it creates a comfortable seating grouping without taking up space visually. Designed by Annie Lawrie Ryerson.

COLOR IT MONOCHROMATIC FOR LARGER LOOKS

Color is probably the most useful decorating tool, especially when it comes to small rooms with confined dimensions. Used correctly and with some skill, color helps to expand space by visual illusion.

For instance, all light or pale shades used on walls help to enlarge the overall dimensions. This is because they recede and seem to push walls out. Pale colors used on the floor create similar visual effects, since they help to stretch floor space by optical illusion.

A monochromatic color scheme is undoubtedly one of the best to use in a small room. A monochromatic scheme is based on one color repeated throughout in its various gradations, going from pale to deep. Because the entire room is filled with the gradations of only one color, a smooth and harmonious feeling is introduced. The eye is not stopped by strong contrasts and all areas of space, plus furnishings, flow into each other for a sense of spaciousness. Choose a color that will not become boring or jarring and it will not overpower the small room.

Obviously all of the light tones and pastel hues are perfect, since they immediately introduce space and airiness. Let's examine some of these.

31

Interior designer Angelo Donghia, A.S.I.D., makes this small bedroom live larger through the use of lots of white and a clever built-in seating area, plus lightly scaled furniture. The designer flashes white paint throughout, not only on walls and ceiling, but on the floor as well. Tables and shutters were treated to white paint too, as was the base of the built-in banquette, right. This was upholstered in white fabric as was the bed's headboard; a white dust ruffle was added to the bed base. All of this white stretches space visually, produces a tranquil mood and makes a perfect backdrop for pretty accent colors of blue, pink and green. Sheets designed by Angelo Donghia for a leading manufacturer are used on the bed, the plain blue-and-white plaid pattern accented by a coordinated pattern decorated with pink and green flowers. This shows up in the quilted spread and the decorative pillows used on bed and banquette. The Parsons table next to the bed provides plenty of surface space, takes up little space visually.

• An all-white room has lots of style and often great sophistication. Today it is possible to use white throughout, because it will look fresh and pristine at all times. The all-white room is no longer a costly proposition in terms of upkeep. Manmade fiber carpets, such as nylon and polyester, spot-clean easily, and many are soil-repellant. Manmade fiber fabrics also wear well, and those treated to a special finish repel staining and soiling. This color scheme will need a degree of balance which can be introduced with pictures, plants, pillows, and other accessories that add vivid accent tones.
• Yellow does a great deal to expand a small room and introduces a bright, sunny feeling. Yellow is best accented with white, apple green, peony pink, and touches of black.

32

• Blue repeated throughout a room produces a cool, tranquil mood while stretching space by visual illusion. However, blue tends to be a cold color, and it is not wise to use it in a room with a north or east exposure which introduces cold light into the room. Blue can be handsomely accented with red, rose, black, white, purple, yellow and green. However, use only one or two of these colors, and be certain the accents blend with each other as well as with the overall blue scheme.

• Green, like blue, introduces a cool ambience, so be careful. Dark fir green used on the walls and floor can be most striking when highlighted with white, peony pink or red. Paler greens may be accented with deeper greens, yellow, white, pink or blue. But blue and green together will emphasize that cool feeling.

• Deep or vivid tones can be used for a monochromatic scheme, but the feeling of spaciousness will be diminished to a degree. However, marvelous effects can be created, especially with red, deep coral and midnight blue. A jewel-box look is introduced when rich jewel tones flash throughout a room. To avoid a spotty look, accent colors should be used sparingly when creating a jewel-toned mood. Black is a good accent with red and coral, while midnight blue looks its best when flashed with white.

This closeup shows the seating area in the bedroom. The built-in banquette forms an L-shape along two walls, and with its plump, white pillows is a comfortable spot for snacks or reading. Decorative pillows introduce color/ pattern interest. Corner is serviced by a white-painted table and a modern wall lamp.

ELEMENTS TO AVOID

There are a few basic elements which you should avoid when trying to expand space by visual illusion. This checklist will help you to recognize some of the more important ones and prevent you from making costly mistakes which can be difficult to correct.

• *Busy Patterns:* These tend to produce an overcrowded and confined feeling when used on the walls because they advance and pull walls inward. They also distract and produce a "noisy" mood. When used on the floor they diminish the feeling of space underfoot, tend to make the floor space look all that much smaller.

• *Too Many Patterns:* When lots of different patterns are splashed throughout a room they produce similar effects to those mentioned above. The mood is busy, and the overall feeling of spaciousness is reduced.

• *Area Rugs:* Most area rugs break up the flow of space visually and create "islands" of texture and color within the room. This makes the floor seem smaller. Area rugs also stop the eye and create a busy look underfoot.

• *Clutter:* Too many accessories used on walls and tabletops produce a cluttered feeling that can often seem messy and overpowering. Eye interest is an important visual element in any room, but too much of it is distracting. Remember, less is more.

2·MAKE LARGER USE OF SMALL ROOMS

Most homes contain one or more small rooms that seem too confined to decorate effectively for comfort and convenience. Yet small rooms do have big possibilities if they are handled with care and imagination.

Through the use of good design, the smallest amount of space can be made to seem much larger than it really is and shaped up to meet a variety of living needs.

Planning is your basic tool, and also the most important. When a room has been decorated using a well-thought-out design plan it will function well, because every inch of space has been properly utilized.

Your initial step is always to make a floor plan of the room. This is easily done by simply measuring the length and width of the floor and then translating these measurements from feet into inches. For information on how to make a floor plan, turn to page 54. Indicate doors, windows, and any other architectural elements, such as a fireplace, alcoves, arched openings, built-ins, sliding or folding doors. It is also a good idea to mark in electrical outlets, light switches and telephones. Show the direction doors swing out and make a note of traffic patterns within the room. Traffic lanes should be about two feet wide, and there should always be about a three-foot clearance at all doorways. Allow about four feet at an entrance door.

The floor plan will show you the amount of space you have to work with and help you formulate suitable furniture arrangements in order to make the most of all available space. It is practical to measure existing furniture or pieces you will eventually be using, again translating the measurements from feet into inches. Draw outlines of the furniture on a separate piece of paper and then cut them out and use the furniture templates, as they are called, to create groupings on the floor plan.

Furniture arrangements should be planned carefully and in such a way that they don't block traffic lanes or make it difficult to enter or leave the room. Through skillful placement the arrangement should make the room live larger.

35

MAKING SPACE GROW

It is worth mentioning here that it's a mistake to think small furniture works best in a small room. This is not necessarily true, and in fact, a room filled with lots of small pieces invariably looks overly cluttered and so appears to be much smaller. However, this does not mean that you cannot make use of some small items which have been skillfully selected.

Furniture that is light in scale, rather than small in proportion, is ideal for a room with confined dimensions. Often a couple of larger pieces can be coupled with standard-sized pieces, and actually might make a striking statement.

The main thing to remember is that you should not include too much furniture as this will create a crowded effect. It also infringes too much on floor space.

TIPS FOR ARRANGING FURNITURE

Almost everyone has problems arranging furniture, and especially in a small room. That is why it is easier to use a floor plan and furniture templates and do it on paper first. This technique enables you to create a variety of different groupings until you find the most effective for your living needs. It is also much less tiring than dragging furniture around a room!

These tips on arranging furniture will help to clarify this particular design element, so that you can produce the best results.

1. Always position large or bulky pieces of furniture against a wall. When such pieces are placed in the middle of a room they appear to be larger than they really are. Generally these pieces are large sofas as well as heavy wood items such as armoires, tables, chests and library tables.

2. Several large pieces of furniture included in one grouping produce an unbalanced look. It is best to separate large pieces to dispense with a heavy effect in one area. This is vital in a small room.

3. Always arrange seating in a pattern that permits traffic flow, and be sure traffic moves around the grouping and not through it. *No less than 2 ft.*

4. Always start a furniture arrangement with the most important or major piece of furniture. Once this is positioned, smaller pieces will fall into place almost automatically.

5. Select furniture that is balanced in height and scale to avoid a "skyscraper skyline" look. When furniture is not balanced it is distracting and introduces a feeling of disharmony.

6. Avoid using lots of small pieces in a small room. They create an overcrowded look.

Project.
Work up
three variations
of a room
One must
have
angles note

36

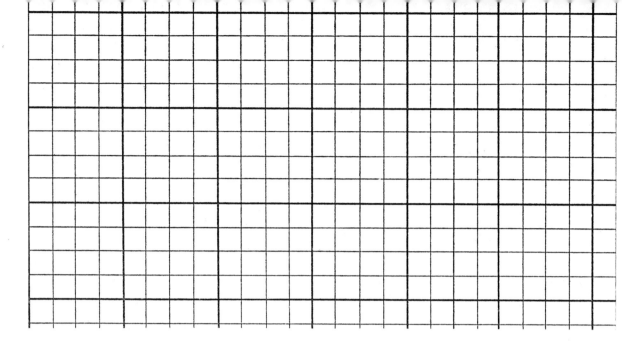

This is the type of graph paper you should utilize when drawing floor plans of rooms. Each square on the paper is a quarter of an inch in size; four squares equal one foot. Graph paper simplifies the task.

This is a typical floor plan of a medium-sized room. Two sofas face each other across a coffee table, are backed up by library tables behind. Two chairs complete the grouping, which is pulled together by the area rug. In the space beyond, a dining table is accompanied by four chairs. Simple outlines like this show you how much furniture you can include and the best places to arrange it within the room. Floor plan by Jane Victor, A.S.I.D.

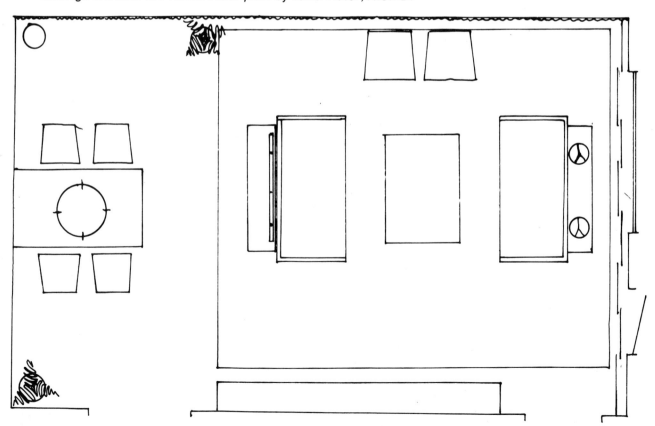

This room was so tiny it seemed to defy good decoration and it had the added disadvantage of being without windows. But Leif Pedersen, A.S.I.D., ingeniously turned it into an office–den with good-looking furnishings, while expanding the feeling of space by covering one entire wall with mirror. Apart from doubling the space in an illusory way, the mirrored wall actually hides a multitude of storage cupboards plus television and hi-fi. Because of the confined dimensions, the designer kept furniture to a minimum but selected handsome pieces that make a strong decorative statement. These include the blue leather Chesterfield sofa, the blue suede-and-steel chairs and the fine wood desk. An Oriental rug introduces jewel colors on the parquet floor underfoot, adding contrast to the basically blue, brown and white scheme. As you can see, the mirrored wall creates a feeling of infinity with its myriad reflections.

7. Do not use too many wood pieces with legs in a small room. Huddled together they introduce a "forest" effect, breaking up space visually.

8. Utilize perimeter arrangements in a small room. This means grouping furniture against the walls rather than in the middle of the room. In this way you will make better use of limited space and free space for traffic.

9. Always select end tables that are of similar height to the arms of

chairs and sofas. Apart from being comfortable, this balanced look creates a feeling of unity and smoothness.

10. Whenever possible, include pieces in a grouping that are dual-purpose. For example, a desk placed next to a sofa and holding a lamp eliminates the need for an end table and lamp, making the best use of space. Similarly, in a bedroom you can use a desk or Parsons table next to the bed, in place of an end table.

11. Select furniture made of similar materials for a small room. For

This second view of the office–den designed by Leif Pedersen shows how tiny the room really is, and pinpoints the false window the designer created, reflected in the mirror. The designer used this decorating device to introduce architectural interest on the bland wall and to simulate daylight through the brilliant handling of mirror and lighting. The window was created by ripping old-fashioned doors off an unused cupboard, and the addition of a built-in base storage cabinet. Louvered shutters front this storage unit and a polished wood top provides display space while simulating a windowsill. The wall above the storage cabinet was lined with mirror; shutters were added above and at either side. Hidden lighting fixtures behind the top shutters produce the effect of sunlight. The door next to the window was also treated to louvers for coordination.

false window

Before its clever revamp by designer Edmund Motyka, A.S.I.D., this tiny bathroom was dingy, cramped, poorly lighted and lacked any storage space. The designer began by remov-

ing the old washbasin with its exposed pipes and wall-hung cabinet above. He also took down the old-fashioned light fixture over the wall cabinet. Cushioned sheet vinyl was used on the floor and taken up to cover the new built-in unit that houses the formerly exposed radiator. Its Mediterranean pattern and earthy brown-orange colors blend well with the white walls and the styrofoam beams which effectively lower the ceiling. Echoing this motif are the oak-look polyethylene cabinets which house the twin washbasins. They form a 48-inch vanity that also hides plumbing and stores linens, cleaning supplies and toiletries. Matching twin mirrors and a ceiling lighting fixture add decoratively and functionally to this area of the bathroom. The small window was visually enlarged by an opaque plastic panel, which lets light in but ensures privacy. Shutters on either side are actually 12-inch wall cabinets that provide additional storage. Without adding an inch to the bathroom's 6'3" by 7'3", a vast amount of space was gained and the room lives more comfortably.

instance, choose wood tones that are the same or which blend smoothly together; and painted pieces that are the same color. Coordinate all upholstery materials using patterns, colors and textures that blend with each other. Wild contrasts are jarring and produce a busy feeling.

12. Consider furniture that is light in scale. This works well in a small room because it appears to take up less space.

13. Furniture made of see-through and shiny materials gives a feeling of spaciousness. Whenever possible, try to include some of these pieces in a small room.

14. Don't overcrowd a small room with too many small furniture groupings. Instead, create one major arrangement that works perfectly for the function of the room. Supplement this with a secondary smaller grouping, if space permits. Another alternative is to utilize an important piece of furniture against a wall for real balance, or consider wall-hung furniture for the same reason.

Once you have made a floor plan and worked out appropriate furniture groupings, you are ready to tackle the other design elements that help to make a small room live larger, such as window treatments, color schemes, wall and floor coverings and special kinds of furniture. A few facts about some of these elements will help you to handle them correctly for the best effects.

Interior designer Michael Sherman provided plenty of comfortable seating and good looks in this minute living room. Secret of the room's success is the U-shaped seating arrangement which caters easily to six or seven and provides lots of color and eye interest. Anchor pieces in the arrangement are the rust corduroy-covered sofa and the two white-lacquered cube tables which flank it. Supplementing the sofa are four ottomans covered in an American Indian print, pushed up flush to the cubes to form the U shape. Cubes also act as "arms" for the adjacent ottomans. A large coffee table provides plenty of surface space. Antique Peruvian jug lamps and an abundance of assorted pillows continue the primitive motif set by the fabric on the ottomans. To balance the interplay of intense tones in the room, the designer painted the walls and ceiling white, used white shade-cloth vertical blinds at the windows. The blinds introduce linear definition and versatile light control, also act as a non-competitive background in combination with the white walls. This designer suggests using tailored window treatments such as this, to dispense with the cluttered look often created by draperies. He feels verticals help to expand space.

GOOD WINDOW TREATMENTS FOR SMALL ROOMS

A window treatment has several basic requirements. It should be decoratively in harmony with the style of the room and the furniture used. It must permit the flow of light and air and provide privacy when needed. In a bedroom, a good window treatment should also have room-darkening qualities.

In a small room these requirements are particularly important, since a poorly handled window can ruin the overall looks. For example, if a window is given an overly elaborate treatment that protrudes too much into the room, the window will look out of place and take up vital space. On the other hand, if the window is dressed with a treatment that is too understated or skimpy it will look lost in the overall scheme of things.

A good window treatment should blend in with the background, color scheme, and general décor, while functioning properly for the room.

In principle, it is best to avoid elaborate or fancy treatments in a small room. For instance, stay away from ornate swags and valances that tend to produce top-heavy effects, especially those of period design. In the same vein, it is wise to pass over very heavy materials such as velvets, thick wools, tweed or fabrics with knubby textures and any others that will make the window protrude into the room too much. Always avoid using dark colors or vivid tones at the window if the walls are paler in hue. Dark colors tend to advance, and when a window treatment contrasts strongly with the walls it appears to leap out. Dismiss strong patterns for the same reason, unless of course the walls have been covered with the same fabric or a coordinated wallcovering.

Instead, consider some of the following treatments, which are most suitable for a small room.

● *Window Shades:* This is one of the best treatments for a window in a small room because it is trim and tailored and fits neatly into the window frame. Today there are any number of styles and colors available to suit almost any decorative scheme. It is also possible to buy window shades in all types of textures which introduce handsome effects. Window shades can also be laminated with fabrics for decorative overtones, and a custom-designed look is easily produced when that fabric is repeated elsewhere in the room. Shades can also be stenciled with attractive motifs or dressed up with stick-on decals.

Because a window shade is made to the exact size of the window it does not intrude into the room or create a feeling of disharmony. A set of windows in a small room can be effectively treated to several coordinated shades, and does not always need to be balanced with another treatment such as draperies or shutters. However, a single window in a small room often requires a supplementary treatment to give it a finished look. This might be short curtains, tie-back or straight floor-length draperies, louvers, shutters, or a lambrequin that surrounds the window. Sometimes it is a good idea to unify sets of windows with a valance, and a valance can also be used to introduce a finished look above a single window in a room.

• *Vertical Blinds:* These blinds are made on a principle similar to Venetian blinds, but with the slats running down instead of across. They have become increasingly popular in the last few years, for a number of reasons. They introduce a sleek, tailored look at any window along with linear interest, and they do not intrude into the room. Since the vanes rotate to create the effects you most require, they also provide the ultimate in light control and privacy. Verticals are available in all colors and lots of new textures to fit various decorative schemes. They look extremely effective when used at long windows or across a wide expanse of glass; they are just as attractive when used on a small window. Like shades, they can be balanced by draperies or left to stand alone.

• *Shoji Screens or Sliding Panels:* Both of these treatments do much to enhance a small room because of their sleek lines, flat design and lack of elaborateness. They actually help to enlarge space by visual illusion since they do not intrude in any way. Shoji screens made of translucent materials filter light well, while creating a decorative look at the window. They also hide radiators and air conditioners and hide an unattractive view, if one exists. Sliding panels work on a similar principle to shoji screens and can be made of wood, metal, or fabric set within wood frames. Open-work grill effects in wood or metal are highly effective since they dress up the window yet filter light and allow air to circulate at the same time. Sliding panels, whether of wood or metal, can be decorated with hand-painted designs for additional impact in a room. Interior designer Jane Victor often utilizes this technique. In a small living room with an updated Egyptian motif the designer covered a window with sliding metal panels hand-painted with ancient Egyptian symbols. They became the decorative focal point in the room.

This designer often uses panel tracks hung with fabric across a window, especially one with a poor vista. Two large panels of fabric hang side by side from ceiling tracks and totally cover the window. One panel simply slides behind the other when daylight is needed.

• *Shutters:* If you want an architectural look at windows these are ideal, whether made of wood or metal. They can be hung singly or in tiers and they will not intrude into the room. Shutters offer excellent light-filtering qualities, and allow air to circulate. They also darken the room very well. Shutters can be used alone, with window shades, or with café curtains.

• *Louvers:* These are similar to shutters and create almost the same kind of architectural feeling. They are usually made of wood, plastic or metal, and since they rotate, are excellent for controlling the amount of air and light in the room. Like shutters, they look best used alone or with window shades or café curtains.

• *Lambrequin:* A lambrequin is composed of three pieces of wood, two of which run down the sides of the window and one across the top to form a valance. A lambrequin is ideal in a small room, since it introduces a decorative look by framing the window without intruding into the room. A lambrequin can be treated to paint, lacquer, fabric or wallpaper. This treatment works extremely well with window shades, floor-length or short sheers.

• *Floor-Length Draperies:* If you want to create a soft look at windows, floor-length draperies are ideal, whether tied back or hanging straight. Those with a French pleated heading help to introduce a feeling of more height. If you want to add a valance, keep it simple in style so that you don't promote a heavy look. Draperies can be used with window shades or sheers and, when privacy is not a major consideration, they can be used by themselves.

FURNITURE THAT EXPANDS THE SIZE OF A ROOM

There are three kinds of furniture that help to expand the horizons of a small room and all are worth considering whether you are decorating from scratch or redecorating.

• *Wall-Hung Furniture* is exactly that, furniture that hangs on the wall and so frees floor space considerably. By going *up* instead of *out,* you are utilizing all the available space in the room to the fullest. Wall-hung furniture is beautifully made and designed today, and comes in lovely woods and finishes, including teak, mahogany, rosewood and walnut.

There are several different systems. Some wall furniture hangs on matching wood panels that are attached to the wall; another type is hung on rails that are also attached to the wall. These ready-made systems can be used to create all manner of wallscapes, since they include quite a few different pieces of furniture. Most systems have shelves, wall cabinets, base cabinets, drop-leaf table–desks, magazine racks and glass-fronted cabinets.

These pieces can provide storage, display areas, bookshelves, and a place for television and stereo equipment. Many of the base storage units provide counterspace to be used as a bar or buffet server. Drop-leaf tables work for dining and also double as desks—for paperwork, card games or hobbies.

• *Modular Furniture:* There are two types of modular furniture—free-standing modular units and seating pieces.

44

Built-ins can be utilized to make any room live larger than it really is, because they take full advantage of wall space. Witness this handsome bedroom where every need is provided for through good planning and a wall of built-in drawers and shelves which store and display. The room was first lined with natural hickory plywood paneling, enlivened by a white ceiling and a beige wall-to-wall carpet. The storage–display wall is composed of floor-to-ceiling shelves made of wood and covered in a high-pressure plastic laminate. Six drawers were made to fit into the base areas, also of wood covered with the natural hickory paneling. The central section has concealed lighting and a storage cupboard that doubles as the bed's headboard, and also provides surface space for books and calendar/clock. Drawers hold clothes, bed linens, records and stationery, while the shelves house everything from television and stereo equipment to books and decorative accessories. To stay with the tailored look of the room, the bed was simply treated to a bedspread and matching pillows. Wicker chair and other pieces used throughout the room, but not shown in photograph, take up little space visually. Designed by Abbey Darer, A.S.I.D.

Free-standing modular units stand flat against the wall. They have increased in popularity in recent years, mainly because of the excellence of the designs now available. Many of these are European imports and they are especially effective in rooms with modern overtones. The modular units include shelves, storage cabinets, drop-leaf desks and tables. Some even come with built-in beds that drop down when needed, and are hidden from sight by closet doors during the day. Since they also go *up* instead of *out*, they free that much-needed floor space for other furniture. These modular units are usually finished in white or rich tones, to suit almost any color scheme.

Modular seating is composed of various pieces that fit together to make an endless number of seating arrangements. Mostly they are armless

45

Modular seating units are ideal for small rooms, since a number of different arrangements can be created to make the most of limited space. In this narrow room, noted furniture designer Milo Baughman uses some of his own modular seating pieces to create an interesting conversation grouping that seats eight comfortably. There are an angled chair and an armless chair on the right side, plus two armless chairs and an ottoman on the left. The two arrangements are linked by a triangle table that fits neatly into the space. A lower triangle table serves as a central coffee table. Two triangle pedestals become a console with the addition of a glass top, positioned on the far wall near the window. Simple window treatment, white walls and bare floor all help to make the room look larger, as does the minimum of furniture. The upholstered pieces are covered in a printed linen velvet in brown, pale aqua and natural. The triangles are in charcoal brown high-pressure laminate.

chairs, chaises and ottomans that can be lined up together to create either L-shaped or U-shaped arrangements. Some systems include a loveseat or chair with one arm; the effect of a long sofa can be created when one of these pieces is used at either end.

Modular seating does much to conserve space because it fits so neatly together for a compact effect. It can also be cleverly grouped to take advantage of odd corners that normally might be lost space. Modular seating comes in both modern and traditional designs, in a variety of upholstery materials, so that it can be used in rooms of all decorative styles.

• *Built-Ins:* Built-in furniture does help a small room to live larger, and if you own your home or know you will be living there for a long period of time, it is certainly worth considering. However, built-in furniture can be quite costly to install, and of course it is not easily moved should you relocate. Obviously it can be ripped out, but you have the cost of doing this as well as the expense of installing it in a new home.

Wall-hung furniture is obviously a great space saver since it climbs the walls instead of intruding onto the floor. In this city apartment living room, designer Peggy Walker, A.S.I.D., used a wall full of storage that is decoration in itself, and some other double-duty pieces. Danish-designed canvas chairs are comfortable and light in appearance, unobtrusive when folded flat. Their natural look in canvas and light beechwood blends with the hand-rubbed finish of the table that also works as a desk, and the wall storage system in walnut. Here just one 11-foot wall accommodates a bar and desk (both with drop-leaf fronts), television, stereo system, loudspeakers, record cabinet, books, shelves and other storage cabinets. All can be moved around at will to suit ever-changing family needs, or just for variety. The sofa in the foreground is a convertible for overnight guests. The bold-patterned, room-size rug emphasizes the floor-free space stretched in size because of clever choice of furniture.

Modular furniture is practical and saves space, as illustrated in this modern living room. This grouping of armless units and ottomans in contemporary styling provides total seating comfort in a small space. The units can be rearranged for parties or entertaining. The added bonus is that the piece next to the tree is a hide-a-bed sofa that opens out into a queen-size bed. The pieces are upholstered in natural and browns, in a woven polka dot.

A whole wall can be treated to built-ins, in much the same way as wall-hung furniture. Shelves, cabinets, drop-leaf tables and desks, plus bar-serving counters can all be included to provide for the ultimate in convenience while saving floor space.

Built-in banquettes are good to use in a room where storage space is at a premium, such as a bedroom, den or children's room. The bases can be constructed as storage units with lift-up lids. The cushions are simply removed when access to the storage space is necessary. Built-in banquettes are useful in a small dining room for the same reason.

A wall of built-in bookshelves with base storage units and a central countertop is highly functional and decorative. The shelves can be filled with colorful books interspersed with attractive accessories and plants. This kind of wall treatment is a marvelous way of introducing visual interest and a focal point in a room without one.

Focal point

48

TIPS FROM TOP DESIGNERS

Most interior designers have to cope with small rooms and make them look and live larger. This they do in a variety of different ways, using clever decorating techniques and tricks. Here are some of their tips.

• Angelo Donghia, A.S.I.D. (American Society of Interior Designers) suggests using one pattern throughout to visually stretch space. He carries it onto the walls and often onto the ceiling; and may even continue the pattern on draperies and upholstery. He explains that one pattern carried throughout produces a smooth, harmonious look, because the eye is not stopped by contrasts.

When he paints the walls of a small room a dark tone he uses a light-colored floor covering or has the wood floor bleached white. When he goes in the opposite direction and paints the walls a light color, he puts down a dark floor covering, preferably one with a mirror-like finish, such as vinyl tile or highly polished wood.

• Jane Victor, A.S.I.D., also uses visual illusion. One of her favorite techniques is to cover one wall with black mirror that reflects and expands the feeling of space without glare. The effect is subtle and soft and makes a good backdrop for furniture. Another idea she uses is the combination of mirror and see-through furniture. For instance, she will cover a whole wall with mirrored panels and then place glass-and-chrome furniture against it, usually two étagères flanking a console. The étagères are filled with attractive accessories and plants, and the double images are highly dramatic. Jane calls this a "floating" wall treatment, since the furniture does seem to float against the mirrored backdrop. It is a great space-expander in a tiny room, and is most effective when the mirrored wall faces a window so that the outside view is also caught and held in the mirror.

• John Elmo, A.S.I.D., pays strict attention to the floor in a small room. He believes a poorly treated floor can diminish space considerably. He cautions against the use of many small area rugs which break up the floor space by creating islands of color and texture. He suggests using one large area rug to anchor a major furniture arrangement and leaving the rest of the floor bare.

He also recommends using a solid-color floor covering, such as wall-to-wall carpet, vinyl in sheet or tile form, or any of the other smooth surface floor coverings. John likes the look of bare, highly polished or bleached or brightly painted wood floors.

49

3·CREATE ROOM WITHIN A ROOM

Very few people have enough rooms to meet all of their specific needs. However, this particular space problem can be solved by making existing rooms function for more than one purpose.

Skillful planning and clever decorating will make it possible to carve extra space from even the smallest area. The room then operates on two, sometimes three different levels.

It is not quite as difficult as it sounds to do this, when a few basic decorating rules are followed. These rules, which are also guidelines, show you how to create another room within a room through the proper demarcation of space, the use of dual-purpose furniture, furniture that is lightly scaled, wall-hung furniture and good furniture arrangements.

Two distinct areas for specific activities can also be created in the one room through well-planned color schemes, selective choices of wallcoverings and floor coverings that will divide the wall and floor areas visually, so that a sense of separateness is created.

For example, many houses and apartments are without a dining room today. Yet it is possible to plan a dining area within a living room, den or even an entrance hall, with a little thought and clever manipulation of furniture. Even when a separate dining room does exist, many people don't want to sacrifice an entire room to dining only. In this instance, it is relatively easy to decorate a dining room so that it functions for other purposes.

Various other family activities put demands on limited space. How often have you felt the need for an office at home, a sewing or hobby corner, a den, a family room, or a home entertainment center? Surprisingly, all of these activities can be catered to by making available space work overtime.

When you have analyzed your exact needs, take stock of all your rooms to determine which one is most suitable for double duties. You might even find that more than one room can be cleverly divided to live as two and so stretch space even further. For instance, it might be possible to create a

This modern living room gets its own separate dining area through the addition of a raised platform at one end. The different floor levels create the feeling of two rooms in one and introduce visual demarcation without interrupting the flow of space. Use of the same sky-blue nylon wall-to-wall carpeting on both levels further contributes to this effect, while the cane-and-chrome chairs and glass-topped table take up little space on the platform, adding to the airiness of the room in general. Placing the sofa flush at the edge of the raised platform reinforces the separateness of the two areas. This platform was relatively inexpensive to make, constructed of sturdy wood underneath the carpet. Three unattractive, oddly shaped windows were treated to colored blinds and the whole area was camouflaged with false plywood walls. These were covered with the same sand-white wallcovering as the rest of the room. Diamond-shaped cutouts of varying sizes permit light to filter in, and produce interesting effects with color and light. They, too, add extra subtle definition in the dining area. The two-color scheme, based on desert sand tones and blue, opens up the room. Plants and pillows add necessary splashes of accent color. Designed by Virginia Frankel, A.S.I.D.

sitting room or office at one end of a bedroom. Then again, a den which has served solely for this purpose might easily be revamped to become a guest room.

Interior designer Angelo Donghia, A.S.I.D., believes that a bedroom does not necessarily have to look like a bedroom. He has long advocated a "sitting room" look, not only for aesthetics and comfort, but to make the ultimate use of all available space. Nowhere does this philosophy show up more brilliantly than in his own bedroom in his New York duplex. When not used for sleeping, this room is in constant use as a sitting room for himself and his guests. The color scheme is a neutral mingling of grays, highlighted by white and sparked by soft accent colors. It has great casual elegance and soothing tranquility. The walls are painted to match the banker's gray upholstery on the bed and sofas, all of which are Angelo Donghia's own designs. The wall-to-wall carpet is also gray to complete the monochromatic shell that allows an infinite variety of changes with accessories. Bright white punctuates the mélange of grays, showing up in the quilted floor-length draperies hung on poles, the tailored, quilted spread, and in all the plump cushions on the bed and sofas. End tables situated in the corners on the window wall are lacquered white. Adding richness to the scheme is a ceiling covered with gold paper. Around the baseboard and molding are strips of silver lamé fabric. The arrangement of furniture is an important facet in the room. The bed is angled across and outward, a pleasing departure from the usual placement of beds, opposite the L-shaped formation of low, upholstered sofas. A low coffee table services this grouping. Accessories are kept to a minimum to avoid an overcrowded feeling; mostly these are paintings, books, plants and flowers, and essentials such as ashtrays and boxes.

This delightful bedroom is not just a place to sleep. It doubles as a second sitting room and a study, and when necessary it is even a place to eat. In essence it is three rooms in one, through the use of clever decorating and skillful choice of furniture and fabrics. Designer Jerome Hanauer picked everything to play a dual role. The white wall-to-wall carpet is luxurious and comfortable, and promotes a feeling of space underfoot. The two unattractive windows were treated to floor-length white curtains and tie-back draperies in a large-scaled floral fabric. The opposite wall was painted white to add spaciousness. The two shorter end walls were lined with a smaller-scaled floral fabric, the companion to the one at the windows. The fabric was first shirred for fullness and then stapled onto the walls at floor and ceiling levels. The bed was successfully camouflaged by adding polished chrome headboards at each end and a quilted, tailored spread specially made to match the draperies. He then positioned the bed against one end wall, instead of jutting it out into the room. Apart from saving floor space, the bed takes on sofa mannerisms with its backdrop of fabric on the wall behind and a collection of pillows lined up against this wall for seating comfort. For storage and extra seating, a pair of low chests were placed side by side in the window area and topped with a cushioned pad covered in the lighter-scaled floral fabric. In strawberry pink and red, the chests can always be used in alternative ways when required and are a prudent choice for long-range decorating plans. The matching campaign-style desk, in white for an airy look, also works for snacks, even twosome dining.

MAKING A FLOOR PLAN

After deciding which room will conform best, your next step is to make a floor plan so that you have an idea of the exact amount of space you're working within. To do this, measure the length and width of the floor space and the height of the walls, using a metal coil-spring tape measure. This is the easiest to use and ensures accuracy. Translate these measurements from feet to inches, utilizing the scale of half an inch equals one foot. Now draw a floor plan on paper, to exact scale, marking in windows, doors and any other architectural elements.

This floor plan is your basic blueprint for your decorating scheme. It shows you all the available space and will help you to define areas for specific activities so that you can decorate them accordingly. A floor plan also indicates the amount of furniture you can comfortably include, and so acts as a buying guide.

Create furniture groupings on your floor plan, rearranging them until you have the ones you like the most and which will best serve your living needs. Don't forget: it is easier moving furniture around on paper than doing it physically!

At the same time you should be considering all the elements that will help you to create another room within a room. Let us talk about some of the most important ones.

FURNITURE WITH A DUAL PURPOSE

There is nothing new about dual-purpose furniture. In fact it came into being in eighteenth-century England, during the Georgian era, one of the most important design periods in history. It was Thomas Sheraton, one of the great master craftsmen of this period, who designed some of the earliest and finest dual-purpose furniture. Sheraton was mechanically minded and created tables that turned into desks, tables that became library steps, the combination bureau-bookcase and desks with secret compartments. His designs show unusual originality and great inventive genius. Rather sadly, Sheraton was not as financially successful as his contemporaries, Chippendale and Hepplewhite, but he gave us a legacy of fine furniture design.

All manner of designs are available today, ones which give a room a double face and stretch space most practically, through the use of single pieces that function for several needs, as well as the highly practical wall-hung furniture.

54

Space problems in this apartment were the need for a study and a dining room. But with only a small living room and one bedroom, these requirements seemed impossible to meet. Designer Peggy Walker, A.S.I.D., solved both by creating two rooms in one. Apart from being the only unused space available, this small entrance was highly practical for dining since it was next to the kitchen. The designer painted the walls of the entrance bright blue to distinguish them from the white-painted walls in the adjoining living room, and to create color impact and a feeling of separateness. She also selected a vividly colored rug, which fits perfectly into the area and also serves to demarcate space visually underfoot. Her solution to the lack of floor space and extra storage space was to use wall-hung furniture in rich walnut. One piece, with bookshelves and storage cabinets, was positioned on the wall just inside the front door; the other, with more shelves and a dining table, was placed on the very narrow wall leading into the living room. The dining table, with a drop leaf, is serviced by two scarlet chairs made of plastic and with pleasing flowing lines. Two extra chairs of the same design and color are simply brought out from the living room when the table has to service four for dining.

When the entrance is not used for meals it easily transforms into a home office, as illustrated here. The dining table doubles as a practical desk with the simple addition of a lamp. The shelves of this system can be moved easily anywhere on the wall rails to suit the needs of the moment. The system is simple to put up and dismantle.

The hide-a-bed sofa is a good space saver in any room, since it is dual-purpose. It provides both comfortable seating and sleeping facilities. Designs have vastly improved in recent years and it is hard to tell a hide-a-bed from any other type of sofa. This one shown here in the living room of a country house has updated looks, with its Parsons-style frame in stark white and floral upholstery in orange, yellow, white and lime. It opens up to sleep two comfortably.

- *Two-Purpose Tables:* Many of the latest dining tables work admirably as desks, or serve another purpose in a room. The simple Parsons table is a good example, as are some of the glass-and-chrome tables. These are ideal to use in rooms which have to double as a den or office as well as for dining. A large circular unfinished wood table, which has been skirted with a pretty floor-length cloth, is an attractive addition to any room. When it is not being used for meals, it is ideal as an occasional table decorated with a lamp, magazines and accessories. When utilizing one of these tables it's a good idea to add a glass top to protect it.

    A table with drop-leaf sides takes up little space when the leaves are down and serves as a console for accessories. It also provides adequate dining space when required. There are also coffee tables designed with an inner-spring mechanism that enables them to be brought up to dining height. Those with drop leaves as well are extremely practical since they help the table to grow in surface space as well as height. It's a good idea to consider all of these tables when planning a dining area within another room.

- *Sofas as Beds:* Of course the hide-a-bed sofa is the ideal piece to use in a den or any room which has to act as a guest room from time to time. All styles are available today and designs have improved enormously. The hide-a-bed sofa works beautifully as a seating unit and turns into a bed very simply by removing the cushions, lifting the mattress up and out.

56

Daybeds, divans and a variety of other styles work equally as well, especially when dressed to look like a sofa during the day. This can be easily accomplished through the addition of a tailored spread, rolled bolsters or back cushions and a mélange of decorative throw pillows.

• *Wall-Hung Furniture:* As discussed earlier, furniture that hangs on the wall saves quite a bit of space. Most of these pieces are designed to function for more than one purpose. Shelves and cabinets that hang on special wall panels provide storage and display space, as well as surfaces for television and stereo equipment. Some arrangements include countertops that double as buffet servers or bars; others have drop-leaf and hinged tabletops that work for dining and desk work. Don't forget that when furniture goes *up* instead of *out* there is more space to include other items, such as chairs, sofas and end tables.

This handsome office was put together at one end of a living room through the utilization of wall-hung furniture and a matching desk. It has a separate, self-contained look and provides for all manner of activities while utilizing only a small corner. The wall-hung shelves and cabinets are suspended on matching panels, and a desk of the same teak fits across the front and out in an L-shape. The desk has plenty of space beneath for readily accessible filing, and the secretarial return helps to keep desktop clear of typewriter and telephone. The desk also works as an extra dining table when required, or as a buffet server for larger parties. The colorful rug helps to define the office within the living room that sees service for all members of the family. Books, artifacts and plants give it decorative overtones, and all can be rearranged at will for different effects.

MAKING SPACE GROW

• *Modular Furniture:* Much of this type of furniture is designed and made in Europe, and is enjoying considerable success here. It is ideal to create a room within a room. Imported by leading distributors, it is composed of various kinds of free-standing units that all come together to cover an entire wall. Some pieces can even be utilized to divide space. These interesting dual-purpose walls can be created by combining display shelves, cabinets and storage units. Some systems come with a bed unit, a great advantage when sleeping space is needed. The unit is actually a cabinet containing the bed, which is concealed by double doors. The doors are opened and the bed simply pulls down for use. When the doors are closed the unit is flush with the surrounding pieces.

• *Audio-Visual Dual Furniture:* Almost everyone wants to include television and music within a room, but often this seems impossible because of lack of space. However, there are certain televisions and stereo systems available that are contained in furniture that sees double use. This includes consoles which act as servers or provide surface space for accessories, while including television or stereo systems in the base. There are also end tables, chests and coffee tables which have the same built-in systems.

DEMARCATE WITH WALL AND FLOOR TREATMENTS

When it is necessary to clearly demarcate areas of space for specific activities, it is possible to do this cleverly and without creating a confined look. For example, you can introduce distinct areas within a room through interesting floor treatments. Two different types of floor coverings will immediately pinpoint two separate areas and will add excitement to any room. Area rugs are especially useful for this. An area rug creates an "island" of texture and color which contrasts with the overall floor and is ideal to define furniture groupings. Or, two rugs can be used at either end of a room to create a similar effect of visual demarcation. Wall-to-wall carpeting can also be given "islands" of color and contrasting texture by adding area rugs.

Another idea to define separate areas is to use wall-to-wall carpeting on only part of a floor. If the uncarpeted part is of a good wood it can be stained dark or painted a light coordinated color; on the other hand it can be covered with vinyl tiles for a completely different look.

Two different wallcoverings can be used within one room to define areas. Interesting effects can be created with patterned fabrics or wallcoverings used in a portion of the room, counterbalanced by contrasting walls elsewhere.

A portion of the room that has been mirrored, paneled with wood,

58

This miniscule alcove at one end of an apartment living room was too small for a dining table and chairs. Yet, because of its odd shape, it was isolated from the rest of the room. Through some thoughtful decorating a library–den was created within the living room. Key to the scheme is the unusual wall-covering, which has an antique gold background decorated with murals of antique maps. These mural panels give the alcove an almost self-contained look. Contributing to this feeling are the built-in bookcase which runs floor to ceiling and placement of the antique reproduction desk and director's chair. A second chair, a footstool and an antique leather box are the only other furnishings used in the area, because of limited space. But the library–den functions admirably as a spot for paperwork and reading or sewing. Warm toast wall-to-wall carpet runs throughout the room, and the overall scheme is a mingling of soft golds and earthy colors.

covered with tiles or patent vinyl appears to be quite separate visually when adjoining walls are treated with other materials. Different colored paints or lacquers used within the one room will introduce a similar look, but remember the colors should be compatible with each other.

When using a patterned wallcovering, always balance it with a coordinated unpatterned wallcovering or paint so as not to create a busy feeling. It is the contrast of colors, patterns or textures that visually defines specific areas.

Add-on architecture can be cleverly utilized to demarcate given areas within a room. Wall and ceiling beams, dadoes and molding used to create

A raised platform was used in this bedroom to create separate areas within the room. The bedroom now does double duty as an office at home and a spot for casual entertaining. The platform and mattress bed is also a comfortable place for sitting as well as sleeping. Wall-to-wall nylon carpeting carried onto the sleeping platform creates a feeling of continuity. The cream-and-brown carpet stretches space, while the walls of rich tan-brown nylon velvet wallcovering introduce warmth. Painted plywood strips crisscrossed on the walls add architectural interest and suggest extra height, as do the white-painted valance and the full-length white draperies. The glass-and-chrome sawhorse desk can be used for paperwork and dining, yet takes up little space because of its see-through qualities. The Lucite side tables also promote the airy look. The platform bed makes maintenance easy—there's no place for dust to collect! Designed by Virginia Frankel, A.S.I.D.

panels all produce unusual effects that add decoratively to the room. Molding can be put up to define an area, while beams used on walls and ceiling can suggest an alcove.

A portion of the room totally lined with bookshelves running floor to ceiling is another architectural trick that defines and decorates at the same time. When shelves cover an end wall and part of the two adjoining walls an alcove is created, and this is most effective as a spot for a sofabed, a desk or even a dining area.

Lavish use of fabrics and some creative decorating ideas carve out an intimate dining room within this sunny all-yellow living room highlighted with rafts of bright red. Key to the room's success is the treatment of the bay window, which transforms into a dining area with the addition of a skirted table and two French chairs covered in a small floral print. Floor-length curtains in a red-and-white mini-check make a smooth, unbroken background for the furniture; while tie-back draperies in a larger red-and-white check frame and define the area. The same fabric appears on the loveseats, with the sides and backs upholstered with the mini-check for true coordination. All of the wood pieces in the room are painted in red, yellow or white for a lighter look, and the glass-topped coffee table adds to the illusion of space in the seating area. Further reinforcing this feeling of openness is the use of bright yellow nylon shag carpeting, which matches the yellow fabric-lined window wall.

CARVE OUT DINING SPACE

Every family needs a pleasant spot for dining and it is possible to create one even when space is at a premium.

The most obvious room in which to create a dining area is the living room. There are several ways to do this. Some are simple, others are a little

61

more complicated but more effective in the end. Which method you decide to use depends on the amount of available space, personal taste and the amount of money you can afford to spend.

When the living room is relatively small it is wise to select a few essential pieces of furniture, such as a dining table and chairs. A rolling cart can always be utilized as a server, hidden in a closet or hall when not in use for dining. These essential pieces should be arranged in an appropriate corner or at one end of the room.

Two things are of prime importance in this instance: the furniture should be light or small in scale, so that it does not overcrowd the room, and it must harmonize with the furniture already there. So pay attention to the style of the dining furniture and the materials it is made from. Be sure that wood tones blend with existing wood tones and that the upholstery on the chairs matches other fabrics in the room and fits the overall color scheme.

It is worth mentioning here that a glass-and-steel table can be used with almost any period of furniture and it blends well with all wood tones, since its see-through materials do not compete. It also appears to take up less space visually and is an asset in a small room. Dining chairs made of cane and chrome or those with white-painted frames also appear to take up less space, making them most suitable for small rooms.

When space is not so limited you can be more elaborate in creating your dining area. However, even with more space available, it's a good idea to use fairly light furniture, and of course the same rule applies about matching furniture styles and wood tones. If you have enough space, you can add a server or a sideboard instead of utilizing a rolling cart.

Should you want to create a feeling of separateness, you can define the dining room in many ways. Highlight the space by using a different wall treatment than used elsewhere in the room; or use add-on architecture; or an area rug that forms an "island" underfoot and pulls the furniture together.

You can also actually divide the room, by using any one of a number of dividers. These include low or high free-standing units that partially intrude into the room; etageres; a set of folding screens covered with mirror or decorative fabric; a buffet server; or a furniture grouping formed to isolate the dining area from the living room. If you have lots of room, you can create a feeling of real division by adding metal or wood gates. A grouping of plants introduces visual demarcation between two areas, without blocking out light. A combination of tall and small plants can be used, the smaller ones placed on small tables of varying heights for a graduated look.

Interior designer Jane Victor suggests two other ways of creating a dining room within another room. In her own apartment, she made a dining room at one end of the living room by adding three floor-to-ceiling pillars

Designer Edmund Motyka, A.S.I.D., removed the wall that separated this kitchen from a small adjoining room, which was too confined to function for anything in particular. The walls were covered with paneling with the look of old wood and the floor highlighted with colorful sheet vinyl in an Art Deco pattern. The attractive bamboo chairs have a dining-room appearance and totally dispense with the kitchen look. They are teamed with a circular table skirted in a floor-length fabric that picks up the rainbow hues of the floor covering. The table itself is made of an unfinished wood top, cut to a specified size and attached to an inexpensive metal tripod base. Plants and pictures, plus attractive light fixtures add touches of elegance to the kitchen–dining room. For larger parties, card tables covered with pretty cloths and folding chairs are utilized to cater to as many as twelve to fourteen guests.

across the end of the room, with enough space between them and the windows for a dining table and chairs. The pillars, Doric columns in fact, were softened with floor-to-ceiling draperies hung in between. These tie-back draperies partially conceal the dining table yet are highly decorative elements in the room. The space behind the pillars was adequate enough for a dining table, eight chairs and a small sideboard. With the dining area situated at one end of the living room, she was able to utilize a small alcove, previously intended for dining, as part of the living room. She gave it the look of a library and linked it to the living room through the use of color, texture and matching furniture styles. In essence, through clever decorating she created three rooms in one.

Jane happens to be a designer who is always having to solve space

In this apartment living room, which measures 35' x 15', interior designer Jane Victor, A.S.I.D., cleverly divided space through furniture arrangement and the use of two different-shaped area rugs. The large square rug creates an "island" in the center of the room and pulls together the furniture grouping that includes two loveseats, two tub chairs and two French chairs, serviced by a steel-and-glass coffee table. Narrow library tables behind the two loveseats hold lamps, and one functions as a writing desk partnered with a chair. The wall-hung shelf saves floor space and provides a spot for accessories. Balanced by a collection of paintings highlighted by panel-track lighting, this wall is the center of eye interest in the area. The circular area rug anchors the glass dining table and French chairs, and this separate corner doubles as a place for card games and backgammon. The traditional chandelier focuses attention on the corner, while floor-to-ceiling draperies camouflage three oddly shaped windows. Étagère and plants round out the corner. Smaller drawing in the bottom left-hand corner shows treatment of the wall opposite the focal wall in the room.

problems, and one of her favorite solutions for rooms that have to double their function is the use of platforms. She often utilizes these raised levels specifically to define dining areas within rooms, and recommends them since they are not costly to create and are very effective.

The size of the dining platform depends on the amount of space being allotted. It must be large enough to hold the furniture with comfort and have enough space for traffic.

Jane constructs the platform from hardwood or very strong plywood and then covers it with an attractive floor covering. Usually she selects something that will contrast with the living room floor. One of her most exciting schemes was a crisp interplay of black and white, glass, steel and other shiny materials. The platform was covered with vinyl tiles with a wet-look patent finish. White vertical blinds were used on the windows, running floor to ceiling to produce a slick backdrop. The furniture included a steel-and-glass dining table, steel-framed chairs upholstered in white kid, and a sideboard made of mirror and black glass in Art Deco style. Portions of the walls immediately above the platform were covered with black mirror, for sparkle and the feeling of space. A crystal chandelier and lots of plants completed the unique scheme, created at one end of a red, white and black living room.

In this charming kitchen designed by Michael Sherman, a newly installed picture window transformed the dark seventy-year-old room into a brighter and more modern one. The brightly colored wallcovering patterned with vegetables helped to open up the area visually. The designer, who had suggested the new window, dramatized it to the hilt and turned it into a backdrop for dining. It was treated to a grass-green window shade trimmed with white, café curtains and valance of green-and-white fabric. The round oak table and antique ladder-back chairs fit neatly into the window area, their rich wood tones adding to the textural/color play. An old wall cupboard was revamped with shirred fabric inserts as a decorative counterpoint to the window, while an antique chandelier adds elegance.

Interior designer John Elmo thinks that space in the typical L-shaped living room which opens up in to a dining alcove is a total waste of space when it is used only for dining. When he has to decorate this type of room he usually prefers to turn the alcove into a library–den, utilizing furniture that can double for dining. In one of his most eye-catching schemes he covered all the walls with floor-to-ceiling shelves, continuing them around the window and filling them with books. Under the window he built a long unit for storage, which also acts as a buffet server when required.

The desk was made from a huge slab of wood, lacquered black to look like ebony and held by two steel sawhorses. This doubles as a dining table and seats six. It is also perfect for buffet suppers. When not being used for meals, the desk is placed immediately in front of the back wall of books, partnered with a high-backed modern, chrome-framed chair upholstered in red. Its companion is positioned on the other side of the desk. These double as host and hostess chairs for dining. Four director's chairs, made of black leather and chrome, form a small grouping at the other end of the alcove, along with a small glass table. These chairs pull up to the desk-table for dining.

Through skillful decorating and careful choice of furniture, the alcove sees double duty around the clock. John suggests using this type of scheme in a separate self-contained dining room, when space is at a premium.

Chicago interior designer Joan Blutter has created many dining rooms in hallways and entrances. She has made even the most miniscule comfortable and attractive spots for dining, and you might consider transforming an entrance if you have one with medium space.

Joan is a firm believer in the use of mirror when space is confined. She also suggests using lightly scaled furniture, pieces made of see-through materials such as glass and Lucite, and folding chairs of clear plastic when space is really short. In this way, your only vital piece is a table. Chairs are simply brought out when needed.

One of Joan's most brilliant decorative schemes was created totally with mirrored panels, which were used on all the walls, doors, and the ceiling as well. The result was a sort of reflective box, where images were doubled, tripled and quadrupled for a marvelous feeling of floating infinity. The floor was covered with black marble, and Joan suggests you can duplicate this look with black vinyl tiles or sheet vinyl, if you cannot afford to put down a marble floor.

The dining table, composed of two glass-and-chrome console tables, each one eighteen inches wide, was a most imaginative idea anyone can duplicate. During the day the consoles are on opposite walls of the hall, one holding flowers, the other a crystal lamp. For dining, one is pushed to the

This entrance hall was transformed into a dining room, gaining beauty and usefulness. Decorated with a minimum of fuss and on a budget, its facelift began by adding three wooden beams to the side wall. The beams were covered with mirrored tiles, the same tiles repeated down the center of the alcove wall for coordination and additional sparkle. The shrimp-colored geometric wallcovering used on the alcove wall balanced the look. A banquette was built-in, made of strong wood and cushioned with loose seating pads and pillows covered with bright shrimp-colored fabric. A matching ruffle disguises the wooden base. A small shelf built behind the banquette provides a spot for necessary lighting and a display area for accessories. The banquette is serviced by a steel-and-glass dining table and steel-framed chairs and stools, which all pull up easily and create comfortable dining facilities for six. The adjoining wall was highlighted with silver wallcovering in a larger pattern, and a long panel of mirror composed of the same mirrored tiles used in the alcove. In combination with the white-lacquered mirror, this wall helps to open up the small area through its sparkle and visual illusion. The white-lacquered console was included in the scheme as a hallway vanity and for extra buffet service.

other side of the room to stand flush next to its partner. In combination the two form a large table which seats six. The duo can be moved into the center of the room to cater to extra guests. With the glass tables, Joan utilized folding chairs made of clear plastic that are easy to store in a closet or in a large plastic bag underneath the bed. A glass-and-chrome rolling cart, with sides that extend, was selected as the server.

There are many other clever ideas which can revive many ignored areas in your home. An entrance can be turned into a cozy and intimate corner for dining. Folding tables and chairs are a good investment, as they are relatively inexpensive and can be brought out easily and set up for meals.

Peggy Walker is a designer who likes to use wall-hung furniture to provide both dining and office space in a hall; selecting those that come with storage units as well as shelves, and feature drop-leaf tables that also serve as desks. Peggy often makes use of these pieces in other rooms, especially when she has to create a sewing, hobby or office corner.

Dining in the kitchen has become very fashionable these days and it seems to be an ever-increasing trend. How elaborate the dining area is will depend, of course, on the space available. There are many small dining pieces that fit easily into odd corners in kitchens; but when space is less limited it is possible to include built-in banquettes partnered with a large circular unfinished wood table, skirted with a pretty cloth. The ideas are endless and some exciting ones are shown in this chapter, all of them created by leading interior designers.

A ROOM FOR SITTING AND SLEEPING

Angelo Donghia is a designer who has done much to change the look of the modern interior, updating its appearance with a more casual kind of elegance. He has long advocated the "sitting room" look for bedrooms, which is extremely popular today. This look is created with the inclusion of living room furniture; long ago Angelo decided to dispense with chests, armoires and dressing tables. He believes these pieces create a furniture storage–room feeling; one that is unattractive, overpowering and unnecessary, since storage today can easily be created in other areas of the home. He also feels that a bedroom decorated to function only as a bedroom is a waste of valuable space.

His own bedroom shown in this chapter is a masterful design in grays and white and looks exactly like a second sitting room. Donghia feels a bedroom should not be off limits to guests, and should be a general living area; a second living room to be used during the day as well as for sleeping.

Interior designer Jane Victor, A.S.I.D., created three specific areas within this bedroom. Taking pride of place in the room is the handsome canopied bed, set against the main wall. In the window area, totally curtained to disguise two unattractive windows, French chairs and a small table form a comfortable seating arrangement for daytime relaxation. Skirted console table behind holds lamps which provide total illumination in this area of the room. Small drawing on the right illustrates the seating–writing corner, actually arranged in a small alcove adjoining the window and facing the bed. Here the designer has used a lightly scaled wicker sofa, French chairs, a Parsons end table and Parsons desk. Because of their trim lines, they take up little space yet provide lots of comfort and convenience for sewing, paperwork and reading. By creating different furniture arrangements within the room, it lives around the clock.

There are many new bed designs available today that simulate the look of large sofas, to help in creating a sitting room in the corner of your bedroom. Or, if you require a desk area for paperwork, there are many space-saving pieces for that too.

To create a sitting-room corner the essential pieces are a chair and table. There are many combinations for this. And your personal tastes and needs will dictate. Obviously, the larger the space, the more you can include, and when spacial dimensions are not confined it's a good idea to include a small writing desk. This helps to round out the arrangment and add real living-room style. At the same time it makes the bedroom double as a place for paperwork.

Music and television can easily be included if you have the space. Many consoles are specially designed for bedrooms and have the look of fine furniture, often being authentic copies of period furniture. If you don't have the space for consoles, a radio on a bedside table and a small television set on an end table or desk might be enough.

Accessories help a bedroom function as a sitting room. Think in terms of pillows for the bed and sofa, colorful pictures or prints on the walls, good lamps, decorative tabletop objects, and even plants and books. Apart from the visual interest they create, they say something about you and your taste and help to stamp a room with individuality.

THE DEN WITH MORE THAN ONE LIFE

The small extra room usually becomes a den, study or library. But if you really want to get the most out of space you should make this room function for a variety of living needs.

For example, a den can easily double as a guest room. All it needs is a bed that looks like a seating unit. The choices are a sofabed, a daybed, a divan or a French Directoire-style bed with head and footboards. The latter type, when pushed against the wall acts as a sofa, especially with the addition of rolled bolsters and pillows.

Of course some storage is necessary in a den that has to function as a guest room. A simple solution is end chests which serve as end tables and offer drawer space.

Wall-hung furniture and modular units are ideal for a den that has to perform in other ways. They free the floor area and offer display and storage space for books, accessories, stereo and television, and all sorts of other items. Some even come with built-in desks and built-in beds, as mentioned earlier. Most have base storage cabinets to hold things like a sewing ma-

Designer Eileen Bickel, A.S.I.D., made formerly unused space work overtime as a place for the pursuit of hobbies, sewing and family entertaining. It also quickly adapts to become a guest room when needed. The designer flashed bright yellow lacquer paint throughout, using it on walls, sloping ceiling and in the window areas, to suggest bright sunshine at all times. Rich color underfoot comes from the carpet of acrylic pile yarns in a mix of gold, bronze and olive. Developed for use in commercial interiors, this carpet is now available to homemakers who want to take advantage of tight construction, long wear and soil-hiding properties that are built in. It is particularly ideal for a room that is in constant use. Reinforcing the sunny effect are built-in fluorescent fixtures and incandescent lamps, which provide plenty of light in what otherwise could be a dark room under the eaves. Sewing and cutting tables of light-toned wood were designed to fit snugly along the window wall. Circular table and director's-style chairs form a small grouping for activities. The seating–sleeping alcove at the far end of the room is a glowing mosaic of color which springs from the patchwork carpet lining the wall of the alcove and the blue-lacquered sloping walls. The designer used carpet as a wallcovering here because it adds textural contrast, warmth and comfort behind the divan, which works for seating and sleeping. Because of the oddly angled wall, it suggests a canopy. The quilted, fitted spread on the divan is in a larger-scaled patchwork pattern in soft greens and yellow, and it contrasts effectively with the carpeted wall. The pillows pick up some of these tones and cleverly bridge the two different patchwork designs. Because of its Plexiglas base, the divan appears to take up less space. It is serviced by two end tables made of Plexiglas.

71

chine, typewriter, records and liquor. In fact, wall-hung furniture and modular units help to turn any den into the room you need—a guest room, a spot for family hobbies or a place for general entertainment.

All of the photographs in this chapter show you how to create that room within a room and make the most use of space. All of the ideas are easy to adapt to your own room sizes, and the captions explaining the pictures tell you why certain decorative themes were used and what they accomplish.

4·DECORATE SPACE FOR TWO CHILDREN

A room that has to be shared by two children can present many decorating problems, especially when the room is small. The basic problem is how to divide the space and yet maintain control of that space within one room.

All children feel they have territorial rights and want their own space for playing and studying, and their own place to store things. And there is the added problem of where to house the occasional sleep-over guest. Apart from all these living needs, there is the need for storage space for winter and summer clothes.

However, decorating problems can be solved and space can be apportioned correctly if you formulate a sound design plan, cleverly utilizing every inch of space. Not only can space be stretched effectively, each child can be given his own fun and decorative domain.

At the outset you should make a floor plan of the room. This is easy to do and it will show you the amount of space you have to work within. For information on how to create your floor plan turn to page 54. This paper floor plan is a helpful tool for allocating space, and shows you the most appropriate areas for furniture. Sketch in furniture groupings, rearranging them until you have the ones which will work best for the children's specific needs; or make paper templates to experiment with furniture placement.

The floor plan will also help you to determine whether or not you should divide the room physically with some sort of divider or do it by visual illusion. Which method you choose depends on the size of the room and how much personal space each child needs. There are various ways to divide a children's room effectively, let's take a look at some of them.

DIVIDERS WITH A DIFFERENCE

The most obvious way to divide a children's room in half is to build a *false wall* made of strong hardboard or plywood, space permitting of course. The

This sunny room for two little girls was skillfully divided into a play area and sleeping area by designer Virginia Frankel, A.S.I.D. Her method: two sets of folding louvered doors and a central divider–storage unit with shelves on both sides. The doors were selected because they do not block out light, yet provide privacy by closing the doors to meet the central unit. For a bright, cheerful mood the designer used a two-color scheme based on a play of bright yellows and white. The walls of the sleep area were covered in a yellow-and-white diamond-checked wallpaper, while the adjoining playroom was painted white for a feeling of separateness. To produce a feeling of expansive, unbroken floor space the designer put down wall-to-wall carpet splashed with yellow and white. A fabric with an Oriental pattern in the same color tones was used for drapes, bedspreads and floor cushions. The doors were standard buys from a lumberyard, painted white and added after the carpet had been laid. The central unit was a simple carpentry job any handy do-it-yourselfer can make. It was given shelves on each side and a base storage cupboard. Painted yellow and white, it is free-standing in the center of the room. The white table is actually a storage box, another easy carpentry project. The Parsons tables that service each bed were unfinished wood pieces, lacquered white. They match the wicker furniture used in other parts of the room.

74

DECORATE SPACE FOR TWO CHILDREN

A room of medium size caters to the living needs of two young girls through careful planning of space, simple yet effective furniture arrangement and a soft color scheme. Interior designer Nina Lee, A.S.I.D., prudently selected furniture that will grow with the ten-year-old girls, so that the room will function well through their teens, even after. The matching beds and storage unit with desk have an antique white finish that introduces an airy, light look into the room. The designer selected this finish since dark woods tend to take up space by visual illusion. The spacious mood is further emphasized by the subtle apple-green walls and white ceiling, while the soft peach carpet stretches floor space, adds warmth. All the furniture was arranged around the periphery of the room, for a neat, compact feeling. Beds placed on adjoining walls, other pieces under the window and on the side wall free the central floor area. With their tailored, quilted spreads and rolled bolsters, the two beds double as comfortable seating units. The same lighthearted floral fabric containing all the colors in the room was used at the windows for the ruffled valance and short tie-back draperies. It also trims the wide window shade that artfully unites the three small windows. With its charming sitting-room ambience, the room works for both girls.

wall would run across or down the room, creating two rooms within one. However, this is not always the best solution, because it can create a confined feeling in both areas and, depending on placement of the windows, block out light from one of the sections. If you are lucky enough to have a very large room with lots of windows, you can use this method. A false wall is not difficult and not too expensive to construct, and it will provide the ultimate in privacy for each child. Obviously the wall should be effectively decorated on each side. Perhaps the kids could decorate it themselves or you can use paint or an attractive wallcovering. An entrance should be created in the center or at one end of the wall, to allow easy access from one area to the other. There are several entrances you can choose from: a standard door, louvered doors, a floor-length window shade, draperies, or even bead curtains.

If this kind of division is not feasible, there are many other ways to divide a children's room in half. A series of *waist-high chests* can be placed side by side down the middle of the room, to create two specific areas. These not only divide without blocking out light, but provide storage space and countertops for toys and books. Inexpensive unfinished wood chests are readily available, and when painted in bright colors they add decoratively to the room's overall scheme. You might consider painting two chests in one color, the other two in a contrasting tone, using the colors as a personal signature to signify which chests belong to which child. This same color signature theme can then be carried out in the rest of the room, on bookshelves and closets.

A variety of different *free-standing units* are available and these, too, divide with ease. The best type to use is those which come with base storage cabinets and shelves rising to the ceiling. Because of the see-through quality of the shelves, light is not blocked, even when toys and accessories are arranged on them. A good idea is to arrange books on the lower shelves so that the higher ones are free for small objects that don't obstruct light.

Louvered doors with shutters that open and close can be effective dividers that are not too costly to install. It is important to select the type with movable slats, to permit light to circulate. Louvered doors that fold back flat against the wall are the best, since these can provide privacy and will open up the entire floor area for play during the day. Interior designer Virginia Frankel sometimes uses louvered doors in combination with a free-standing, narrow unit placed strategically in the middle of the room. The doors close to meet the unit, to create two separate areas when necessary.

California designer Joyce Vagasy is an advocate of *window shades* for dividing children's rooms. Joyce hangs a series of these side by side on the middle of the ceiling and they are simply pulled down to the floor when division of the room is wanted. She uses three to four shades, depending on the size of the room, each identical in style and color, and usually laminated with a fabric used elsewhere in the decorative scheme. For a fun effect, Joyce suggests using shades in alternate solid colors, such as one yellow and one green and so on, or shades stenciled with pretty designs. Decals can also be stuck onto the shades for interesting effects. This designer points out that the shades must be laminated on both sides, since they are being viewed from both areas of the room.

Sliding panels similar to shoji screens make good dividers, especially when the material used is translucent to permit light to penetrate. Panel tracks attached to the ceiling and holding sections of colorful fabric also work well and are simple and inexpensive to create. Doubled fabric must be used for each panel, and they should be floor to ceiling for real effectiveness. A wand mechanism (a small hanging rod) is attached to the end panel enabling you to slide one panel behind the other when total division is not required.

LESS THAN MEETS THE EYE

Interior designer Jane Victor, a mother herself, likes to divide children's rooms by visual illusion. One of her techniques is to create two separate areas within the room through the skillful use of color. One clever idea she often utilizes is to paint a broad stripe of color down the middle of the main wall, repeating this on the opposite wall. An identical stripe of vinyl, in the same width and color, is run across the floor to meet up with the wall stripes. This band of color promotes a sense of visual demarcation and each child is given half of the room. Jane sometimes paints these adjoining sections different colors to define space for each child, but she unifies the rest of the room with white-painted furniture and coordinated fabrics.

Jane points out that children, like adults, have an emotional response to color, and suggests that attention be paid to their color preferences. She has discovered that most of the children she has decorated for like explosions of vivid color and find these schemes exciting and fun.

Placement of furniture often demarcates by illusion. For example, beds positioned in opposite corners of the room will give each child his own personal area, while leaving central floor space free for other activities. When this method is used, chests or wall-hung furniture should be used in combination with each bed to further fulfill the self-contained look.

Étagères can serve as visual dividers. Buy ones made of Plexiglas or Lucite. These materials are ideal for a children's room since they won't dam-

Gordon and many other characters. The white wood furniture has been enlivened with color accents that pick up the vivid red, yellow and blue hues from the carpet. This has a practical as well as decorative aspect. The signature stripes of yellow and red on closets and chests identify each child's own storage units. These same colors line the shelves to individualize areas for storing books and toys. One yellow and one red blanket on the bunk beds reiterate this personal signature theme, and the carpeted wall behind adds soft texture and sound insulation as well as lively pattern. The carpet has anti-static and soil-resistant properties that make it ideal for children's rooms. Also, its tight construction ensures toughness and durability as well, while foam backing dispenses with the need for under-padding. Bunk beds have wall-mounted lighting fixtures, and extra lighting is included on the chests. The latter were unfinished wood pieces painted to blend with the room, and they make a sturdy base for the shelves constructed of wood, also dressed up with spray-on paint.

Designer Peggy Walker, A.S.I.D., drew her inspiration for this cleverly divided room from a new "comics" carpet, an allover print depicting such cartoon characters as Blondie, Henry, The Katzenjammer Kids, Daisy, Flash

age easily and don't take up space visually. The étagères should be placed in the center of two facing walls, jutting out into the room at an angle. Each child is given an area of his own on either side of the étagères. These pieces of furniture also provide shelf space for displaying and storing possessions.

SPACE-SAVING FURNITURE FOR CHILDREN

It is not always possible to divide a children's room in half, either physically or visually; nor is this always desirable. But you can make one room work well for two children by apportioning space carefully and by using space-saving furniture.

The beds are obviously of prime importance and should be your first consideration as you make your decorating plans. Today you have a wide choice of children's beds in all styles and price ranges. The majority of children like bunk beds, and these take up the least amount of space in a room because they go up instead of out. Atttractive designs in a variety of materials are available, and, of course, there are the unfinished wood bunk beds which can be lacquered or painted any color you wish.

Interior designer John Elmo, the father of two, suggests treating each bed in such a way that it doubles as a seating unit by day. He recommends the use of a fitted spread, or one that neatly tucks in, plus rolled bolsters and pillows. These are easy to remove at night and can be stacked in a corner or stored in a cupboard. In this way the beds become dual-purpose and help to free floor space for desks and storage units.

North and South get together in this bright, cheerful boys' room featuring a Civil War theme in the lively, patterned wallpaper. When one brother wants to secede from the Union, he merely rings down the ingenious ceiling-hung shade used as a room divider between the beds, made of the same textured cloth as the window shades. For a handsome touch, all three shades boast crenelated borders and gold-finished café curtain rods as bar-pulls. Smart cadet-blue bedspreads sustain the tailored theme in tones of cornflower trimmed with navy, while the vivid tangerine shades deliver the contrasting punch. Beds are angled in an L-shape to fit neatly into the miniscule room. A do-it-yourself desk-shelf exploits the natural light and the normally wasted space beneath the windows, providing an ample work-and-study area for two. Stools, window frames and rug are cornflower blue; the vinyl floor, white and washable. The large gilt eagle and the Victorian clock add appropriate Early American accents. These decorating ideas work equally as well in a girls' room.

Jane Victor always examines built-in closets in a room designed for two children, since these can often be converted into alcoves for bunk beds. For example, in a recently completed scheme she transformed a large recessed closet into a sleeping area which did not intrude on much-needed floor space. The doors were removed and bunk beds fitted into the space. The walls of the closet and the bunk beds were lacquered in bright colors and the sleeping alcove was then framed with a valance and tie-back draperies.

Trundle beds also save space, since the lower bed slots under the top one, when not in use. When the top bed, which is always visible, is treated to bolsters and throw cushions, plus a tailored spread, it then serves as a seating unit by day.

When a trundle bed is used in combination with a built-in bed, sleeping facilities can be provided for two children, plus the occasional guest. Designer Carl Fuchs used this idea in a dormitory bedroom he created for two sisters. The scheme began with the built-in bed—actually a raised platform rising up the wall and supported by two solid storage pedestals. A single bed was positioned on the platform and treated to look like a seating unit, while the trundle bed was fitted into the space underneath the platform. The trundle simply pulls out to sleep one or two. A set of steps provides easy access to the sleeping platform. By day, the trundle pushes underneath the platform to conserve floor space.

Apart from sleeping facilities, children require work-and-play areas, as well as storage space. Whether space is at a premium or not, wall-hung furniture is one of the best solutions because it caters to all these living needs and produces a neat, compact look within the room.

It is possible to create many different combinations with wall-hung furniture, all of which offer display-storage facilities as well as study areas. Most of the latest wall systems contain a variety of individual units that can be assembled to create any type of arrangement you wish. Shelves, small wall cabinets, larger base cabinets and drop-leaf or built-in desks are all available and can be arranged at will on the wall.

Free-standing modular units that stand against the wall also work well in children's rooms. They provide closets for clothes, storage chests, shelf space, as well as compact desk areas for two. One unit comes with a bed built into a closet, which pulls down when the doors are opened. This type of unit is worth considering to provide sleeping facilities for sleep-over guests. Another unit contains twin beds behind closed doors. This, of course, is ideal for a room shared by two, since it dispenses with the need for beds which take up floor space.

Both wall-hung furniture and modular furniture are prudent buys, since they grow with the children and can be used through their teens. Since

A bedroom shared by two children in a country house features a large sitting room and play area, plus two small curtained alcoves for sleeping. The alcoves were created through the simple addition of a false wall, and overhead dropped beams that align the alcoves with the fireplace wall also reiterate its architectural overtones. The newly divided space was painted white and treated to homemade platforms for the mattresses. Full-length curtains were added for privacy. The ruddy brick color of the fireplace wall is balanced by a rich red carpet that covers the entire floor area and also upholsters the bed platforms. The plush nylon carpet provides warmth and insulation plus soundproofing. Each bed is serviced by a see-through Plexiglas cube table, and the same tables are used in the play area. Other furniture includes durable lightweight metal-and-canvas chairs. Bold fabrics on the mattresses and seating cushions add rafts of related colors in a room designed around tones of red and white.

these types of furniture are mostly contemporary and tailored in design, they blend well with any decorative scheme, for children of any age. Wall-hung systems are usually in natural woods, while the modular systems come in a variety of solid colors. To my mind, white modular units are the most useful since they are neutral and will therefore suit any color scheme.

A typical attic before its transformation into a room that functions sufficiently for two children.

See-through furniture (glass, Plexiglas and Lucite) and lightly scaled furniture of simple design are space-savers and can be utilized in children's rooms, although these materials may be a bit delicate for the very active.

As mentioned earlier, the placement of furniture is vital when you are decorating a room shared by two children. Individual corners can be created which service each child, so that the central floor area is left free for general activities. It is wise to position pieces against the walls, as obviously all peripheral arrangements leave the middle of the room free for games and other activities.

DESIGNER TIPS THAT MAKE SENSE

Interior designers are constantly faced with the problem of making one room function for two children, and making the space available work well to please both. Here are some designer tips that you might find useful when dividing and conquering space problems in a children's room.

• Jane Victor says that an ordinary built-in closet can double its value in a room, if you raise the hanging rods for clothes and add two small, inexpensive chests. Raising the rods frees space for the chests, which would otherwise take up floor space in the room itself. A small stepladder can be used to reach the clothes.

• Joan Blutter suggests using drop-leaf tables hinged to the wall. When not in use they take up no space at all.

• Peggy Walker often utilizes the space usually lost under a window by adding a long shelf, wide enough to work as a desk or a spot for games. This is attached to the wall with brackets and is serviced by two stools or benches. This only works, of course, if there are no radiators in front of the windows, as in many apartments.

• John Elmo makes a wall work overtime by adding a cork bulletin board or pegboard to hold all sorts of things. Each child gets a bulletin board in a different area of the room, which is painted a bright color.

82

DECORATE SPACE FOR TWO CHILDREN

After clever remodeling by interior designer Louisa Cowan, this attic becomes a charming room for two. Batt insulation was packed between existing ceiling joists, then nailed on furring strips at right angles to which pre-finished, wood-grained ceiling planks could be stapled. The columns and beams are non-structural and cost less than solid beams. The room's focal point is a "raft" swing which was hung so that it could be lowered to accommodate a child's height. When anchored to the floor by chains, it becomes a worktable or a platform for a sleeping-bag bed. Resilient tile floor beneath the swing is designed for easy do-it-yourself installation. The twin built-in beds with storage bins at the bottom sit at each side of the raised area, built on a platform of joists covered with sheet plywood. The colorful floor covering is composed of foam-backed orange-shag carpet tiles, also easy to install because of their self-adhesive backs. Foam mattresses four inches thick are covered with vivid bedspreads; the whimsical pillows are home-sewn fish made from scraps of felt. Picket fences make clever and economical headboards, and are also used over the window where they are hinged to open like a gate. Storage bins make use of space under the window. The five-drawer desk is wide enough for both children and can be built easily and economically by anyone skilled at carpentry. Cubes, half-cubes and drawer units are of molded plastic, as are the stools. Wall-hung shelves (not shown) provide storage space for books, magazines, toys and games. The trees are simply cut from a sheet of Masonite and painted.

5·SPACE STRETCHERS FOR ONE-ROOM APARTMENTS

The studio and the one-room apartment are probably the most difficult of all homes to decorate. It is simple to gather a few pieces of furniture and a bed, to provide the basic necessities. However, in the end, this kind of haphazard decorating is a waste of time and money. Within a few weeks, most people are bored with the look, as well as highly dissatisfied from a function and comfort point of view.

So it is wise to formulate a well-thought-out plan at the outset, providing for every living need with the most appropriate and effective pieces of furniture. This plan is your basic blueprint for the total design and will help you avoid costly mistakes. And if you can't afford to buy everything at once, the blueprint will be a valuable shopping guide to follow religiously.

A one-room apartment or studio has three basic needs. 1. It must function well for all living needs around the clock; 2. it should be attractive and comfortable; 3. it must *not* be visually overpowering. Keep in mind that you will be living in this one area of space all the time, and it must satisfy your tastes and your aesthetic sense, as well as meet your living requirements.

Pay special attention to color schemes and select the ones you *know* you can live with for a long period of time. Avoid unusual, strong or dramatic colors, even if you like them. These are fine in small doses or when used in a home with enough rooms to escape. Also, stay away from drab or dark colors, as these too can quickly become depressing. Don't forget, we all have an emotional response to color and it's wise to select those that promote a happy, relaxed mood.

Resist using lots of patterns within the limited space of a studio or one-room apartment. These can produce a crowded, often busy look and will quickly get on your nerves. Of course, one or two light, airy patterns can be both appropriate and effective when used intelligently; but don't overdo it with patterns.

The same rules apply to floor coverings. Any busy, wildly patterned or

Designer Robert C. Simon makes the optimum use of space in luxury one-room apartments. Each apartment consists of 626 square feet, with the living space, excluding kitchen and bath, measuring 29' x 14'. The individual occupants have different living requirements but basically the same need for dining, living and sleeping space. Simon illustrates a most efficient approach to space planning by using modular wall systems throughout for flexibility. Created for two roommates, this yellow-and-white scheme has distinct living, dining and sleeping quarters all within the one area of space. A display and storage cabinet serves as a room divider and separates the living room and dining area. Maximum seating in the living area is achieved by using an overstuffed, upholstered sofa against the window wall, plus two upholstered chairs on the opposite wall. Placed at right angles to each other, they are separated by a white plastic laminate side table. All furnishings, including the wet-look vinyl upholstery, occasional furniture and modular units, are easily wiped clean with a wet sponge and mild detergent. The free-form Plexiglas coffee table also serves as an auxiliary bar and magazine rack.

MAKING SPACE GROW

This is a second view of the same one-room apartment. A light, airy feeling was achieved with the bright, sophisticated color scheme of yellow and white. All the furniture is white, while the shag rug and the walls are yellow. Painting the wood floor in broad diagonal white and yellow stripes gives the illusion of more space, as do the large yellow, orange and white graphics, stretching the illusion further. The dining area behind the room divider is just off the kitchen. The table can be used flush against the divider, as shown, or pulled back further to accommodate more people for dining in this dual dining/sleeping area. Beaded curtains along the window wall allow maximum light penetration but no invasion of privacy. A TV and stereo are enclosed in the cabinet, with speakers placed strategically so that sound can be heard throughout the apartment or isolated to one particular area.

This is the third view of the same one-room apartment. At night, two single beds which have been concealed in deep cupboards come out from behind closed doors. These deep cupboards also provide the additional closet space that this situation requires. However, each of these one-room apartments contains the standard three closets. The dining area can become a work corner for one roommate, while a drop-leaf desk, which can be used as a bar in a pinch, pulls out of the bed wall. Within the writing area, there is a safe for documents and an inset for letters and papers. The oak-cane-and-chrome chairs add a touch of warmth that wood always conveys. For the most part, all of the furniture selected was modular in design, and in no instance was a convertible sofa used to provide sleeping facilities. Of course, this does not mean that you cannot substitute a sleep-sofa in the living area to accommodate a guest.

vividly colored product is going to make the floor space seem smaller because it reduces space visually.

Investigative shopping is the key. Make a tour of your local stores to ascertain what's available. You have a wide choice in a variety of price ranges. Wall-to-wall carpet provides the ultimate in comfort. A solid color, especially a light one, will stretch space by optical illusion. Many of the manmade fiber carpets, nylon, polyester, acrylic, polypropylene olefin, are especially hard-wearing and easy to maintain, certainly a major consideration for one-room living. They are available in lovely colors and different textures. Vinyl (sheet or tile), asbestos tiles and linoleum are all suitable for one-room studios as are plain wood floors or painted wood floors.

At the same time that you are shopping for floor coverings, it is a good idea to view some of the newest furniture designs. Obviously dual-purpose furniture, wall-hung furniture and modular units are ideal for the one-room apartment, since all of these save space. Like everything else, furniture must be carefully selected because it has to provide the ultimate in comfort and function, as well as look good every day.

Make a floor plan of the apartment. See page 54 for simple instructions for how to do this. The floor plan indicates the amount of available space, and pinpoints areas for different furniture groupings.

FLEXIBLE FURNITURE ARRANGEMENTS

The way you arrange your furniture in a one-room apartment is vital. Good furniture arrangements help to make the most of the available space, while bad ones may diminish space considerably.

In most instances it is wise to plan furniture groupings against the walls of a room, to free the floor space and allow for easy movement within the room. Also, this will promote a more spacious look.

Clever manipulation of space turned this one-room studio with a sleeping alcove into a comfortable environment for living, sleeping and entertaining. Jane Victor began by allocating and dividing space into three distinct areas. She turned the small entrance hall into a dining area (see floor plan), dividing the room with a see-through steel-and-glass étagère between the entrance and the living room. A sliding shoji-type screen covers the entire window wall, and the large area rug anchors the seating pieces into a coordinated grouping. Under the window a long built-in unit spans the entire wall, providing much-needed storage in the studio. In the dining area, not shown on the drawing, a circular table is partnered with French chairs. The chandelier above focuses attention on this area of the long room, and provides adequate lighting.

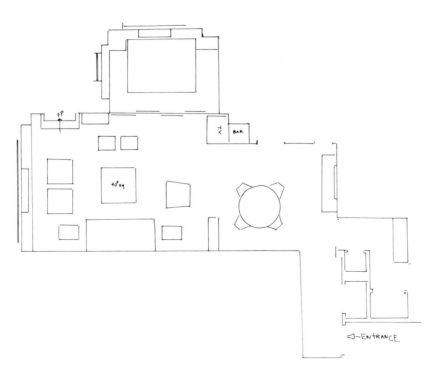

FP

BAR

18'sq

◁—ENTRANCE

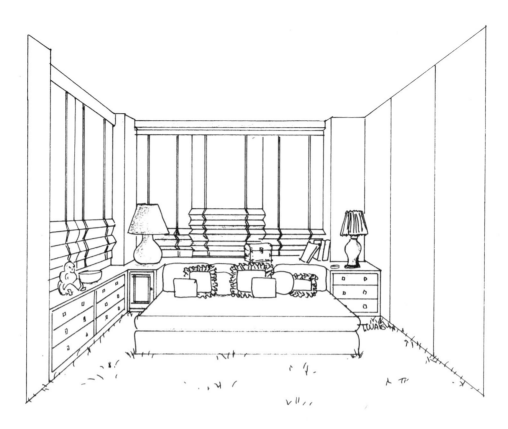

Here you can see the sleeping alcove, which opens off the living room on the wall facing the sofa. There are Roman shades on the two window walls and the third wall holds closets which have been totally covered with mirror for an illusion of extra spaciousness in the room. The bedside chests are actually part of a long storage unit which runs under the window and also serves as a low headboard. The designer closed off the entrance to the alcove, which was without doors, through the use of folding, sliding screens, mirrored on both sides for illusory effects.

SLEEPING AND SITTING

Your most important concerns will be groupings of furniture for sleeping and seating, so you should pay careful attention to them as you formulate your plans.

In most one-room apartments, especially those with limited space (since some can be quite large), the major piece of furniture is the sleeping–seating unit itself, whether this is a sofabed, divan, daybed or period-style bed with head- and footboards.

The sofabed should be placed against a wall, preferably a large wall, and then balanced by small pieces such as end tables, chests, a loveseat, chairs, or benches if you have the space.

SPACE STRETCHERS FOR ONE-ROOM APARTMENTS

Although cramped for space, it is not necessary to be cramped for style as proved by designer Ginny Gray. Maximum impact is achieved in this one-room apartment by the interplay of no-color colors, such as gray and white in textures and finishes, plus various shades of peach in the multi-patterned fabrics. A "floating" wall has been created to separate the dining/living area from the sleeping area, by combining various modular wall units that stash, stow and store everything from china and linens to clothing and stereo equipment. Additional units are used ingeniously to frame a daybed, covered in multi-colored stripes, floral and lattice prints. Colors are echoed in the wall-to-wall carpeting, as well as the shag area rugs. Maintenance is always important and especially so in a one-room apartment, therefore plastic laminated furniture surfaces and quick-cleaning carpet fiber are highly practical. The lattice print of the fabrics and the lattice design of the dining chairs pull the two areas together visually.

Country casual can be warm, informal and appealing, as illustrated in this updated Early American functional studio apartment. Designer Virginia Perlo cleverly planned and divided space in order to provide all the necessities for comfortable living, combining traditional American furniture with some contemporary touches. The rich wood tones of the furniture contrast effectively with the white upholstered sleep-sofa and the highly colored throw pillows. Built off the floor for ease in moving and cleaning underneath, the traditional but updated furniture is teamed with a pleasant mixture of accessories. A bad view is obscured and a decorative touch added by inserting antique stained-glass windows. An antique Americana collection, storage areas for books and stereo equipment are all housed in bookshelves. An étagère is used not only to display additional collector items, but also acts as a room divider between the living and dining areas. The rich tones of the Oriental rug are reflected in the glass-top coffee table, which can be easily moved at night, so that the sleep-sofa can be pulled out. A red leather swivel rocker provides extra seating and promotes the feeling of a serene reading corner. All furnishings can be utilized later in a larger home—whether it be living room, den, guest room or bedroom.

You should include a coffee table to service these pieces and to round out the grouping; but be sure it is lightweight so that it can be easily moved at night. This is particularly important if you are utilizing a sofabed which has to be opened up into the center of the floor. You don't want to be dragging around heavy furniture.

If you're lucky enough to have plenty of floor space and can provide both a sitting and sleeping area at separate ends of the room, always select a bed that can function as a sofa. If using a real bed, dress it up with a tailored spread, rolled bolsters and pillows, to dispense with the bedroom look and to encourage people to sit.

When creating this type of sleeping area it's a good idea to include one or two end tables and a coffee table. This will provide a place for a lamp, a necessity at night, and other decorative accessories; and will also help to create another comfortable conversation area.

CREATING A PLACE TO DINE

Once you have formulated your sitting–sleeping arrangement, consider your other living needs. Obviously a dining area is important, and you might need a work–study area also. You can often select a dining table that also doubles as a desk when needed, and so save floor space. There is more about this on page 54.

If it is feasible, the dining corner should be fairly close to the kitchen for easy service. Bear this in mind if you don't have the space for a server and will be carrying food in and out on a tray. A rolling cart is invaluable in this situation and works well as a server. If you have the space, a dining table can be set up in the traditional manner, accompanied by chairs. If that is impossible, a table alone can be used, decorated with magazines and flowers, and the chairs positioned in other parts of the room. Or they might even be part of a seating grouping, if suitable in style.

A study corner is simple to create, the basic ingredients being a desk, a lamp and a chair. Make use of the wall area near the desk by adding shelves for books, plants and accessories. They will help to fulfill the "den" mood and also introduce a change of visual pace while offering storage space.

WHERE TO STORE THINGS

You must have adequate storage places for all those necessary items that make a home run well, not forgetting clothes and bed and bath linens. Some

93

MAKING SPACE GROW

apartments have plenty of built-in storage cupboards and closets, but if not, be sure to include other types of storage in your furnishing plan. Whenever possible, utilize chests in place of end tables and consoles for added drawer space. Also consider some of the wall-hung systems of shelves that come with roomy base cabinets—ideal because they do not intrude on floor space.

SHAPING SPACE

Apart from the choice of furniture, the way you arrange it is vitally important in a one-room apartment, as pointed out earlier. Basically all arrangements should be flexible, permitting simple regrouping when necessary. For example, a seating arrangement should not be so "set" in position that chairs cannot be moved when necessary, or extra chairs cannot be added to cater to guests. Obviously the sofabed must remain in position, but the other seating units should be movable without spoiling the look of the overall arrangement. If possible, the furniture grouping for dining should also be flexible.

STRETCH SPACE WITH COLOR

A good color scheme is your best friend when you are decorating a one-room apartment. As I pointed out earlier, certain colors help to broaden the horizon of any room. This is a major consideration in one room that has to

Angelo Donghia designed this elegant one-room apartment using sheets that he designed throughout. The apartment attains a look of serenity and togetherness through the use of magenta on all walls and the lovely undulating print on the sheeting in various shades of blue, violet and teal. Draperies made from the same sheets, simply hemmed top and bottom, hang from white wooden dowel drapery rods and are tied back to let in the light and a lovely view of the garden. At night the tie-backs are released and the room becomes an intimate setting for a musical soirée, dinner, and finally for sleeping. The antique piano strikes the right note with its richly mellowed wood finish. The bed, which is quilted at both ends in cream satin, acts as a sofa during the day. Dining usually takes place around the skirted table at the side of the sofa. The table is draped in a fabric to match the wall color and is complementary to the print of the sheets. A long-haired Flokati rug defines the living/sleeping area and adds to the posh feeling of the room. Several armoires serve as storage (not shown in photo). Space is conquered and stretched by the use of quiet, refined, sophisticated colors and the repetition of the same pattern throughout, subtly punctuated by a clear Plexiglas coffee table, unobtrusive yet functional and practical.

serve for all manner of living needs. When considering color schemes for your one-room apartment, think in terms of all the lovely light shades such as primrose, apple, sky blue, cream, pale apricot and, of course, white—for walls as well as floors.

It is wise to stay with a one- or two-color scheme, because both of these promote a sense of tranquility and help to make the most of space. When a room is filled with too many contrasting colors the eye is distracted and space is also reduced by optical illusion. Too many colors juxtaposed against each other in one area of space create a "noisy" ambience that is jarring.

- A *monochromatic scheme* is ideal for one-room living, because it not only helps to stretch space by illusion but also pulls seemingly unrelated objects together for a smooth, harmonious look. For more detail on selecting colors, turn to page 31.

- A *related scheme* can also be used to produce a refreshing yet restful effect in a room. A related scheme is created by using colors which are adjacent to each other on the color wheel. For example, you could select yellow, then add yellow-green or yellow-orange, depending on your preference. On the other hand, you could go in the opposite direction on the color wheel and pick green-blue, adding yellow. A related scheme gains in visual interest when the value and intensity of the colors are varied.

This one-room apartment was designed by Robert C. Simon for a couple who have occasional weekend guests. It can actually accommodate four. Mirrors along half a wall extend the illusion of space, with plants and furnishings reflected ad infinitum. Being independent of the wall, modular wall units change the area by dividing the space at will, adjustments made to suit personal needs. In addition to a queen-sized bed that is part of the wall system (although not visible in this photograph it is on the wall opposite the mirrored wall), the living area's custom-designed seating units provide auxiliary sleeping facilities. All finishes and furnishings are easy-clean, easy-care, thereby keeping maintenance to a minimum. The almost all-red décor is complemented by the dull silver mylar upholstery on the two sofa units which create a seating area, relieved by the white leather chair, a white light column, plus white flowers. The low divider units behind the sofa units provide a sense of privacy. Red casements at the window wall, along with the stainless steel-slatted blinds, allow maximum light penetration with minimum loss of privacy. Plants, paintings and accessories further express the avant garde tastes of the occupants. For entertaining, a bar unit is provided and a movie projector and screen are concealed within the cabinets, as are TV and stereo. More important, when you move, everything moves with you.

SPACE STRETCHERS FOR ONE-ROOM APARTMENTS

Another solution for the living, dining and sleeping problems of one-room living was devised by Robert C. Simon for an executive. The space is identical to the one-room apartment he designed shown earlier in this chapter. Since the main area is an undivided expanse of space, this apartment can be used to entertain large groups of people if necessary. A sophisticated ambience is created by the use of brown throughout, including the wall units and vinyl-suede upholstered sofas. The walls are painted white. This excludes the far wall, reflected in the mirror. Here broad stripes of color such as brown, burnt orange, black and taupe create visual interest. Cabinets conceal a single bed, a sight and sound center including TV, stereo, movie projector and screen, a bar, a desk, and clothes storage. Illustrated here is the trend for the bedroom to be included, to an even greater extent, within the living area so as to achieve better utilization of available space. A unique coffee table made up of four white light balls supporting a glass top provides light and color relief, also displays precious objects such as marble obelisks and shells. Although no draperies or curtains are used, the stainless-steel, thin-slatted blinds control the light admission efficiently.

If you do not like the pale or light color ideas just mentioned, select earth tones, from terra-cotta to desert sand. All the natural shades, such as cement, stone, beige, sand and coffee can be combined to make a room a mélange of truly soft color that is restful. These colors are also an ideal background for brighter accent tones.

SPACE-STRETCHING FURNITURE

There are many kinds of space-stretching furniture. The best types for one-room apartments are discussed briefly here, for more detail turn to Chapter Two.

• *See-Through Furniture:* This type of furniture has been mentioned quite a lot in previous chapters, simply because it is so marvelous for stretching space by visual illusion. For that reason it is certainly highly suited to one-room living.

See-through furniture is actually furniture made of see-through materials, such as glass, Plexiglas and Lucite. When these materials are combined with chrome, steel or brass the look is light, airy, floating almost.

See-through materials in combination with metals are neutral. They do not compete with color schemes, wood tones, wall or floor coverings or any other decorative elements in the room. This is a point worth noting when

99

MAKING SPACE GROW

Maximum effect is obtained in the minimum of space in this studio through the clever use of color, shape and texture and by careful planning to obtain total function. The walls painted in a warm terra-cotta are complemented by the darker brown in the corduroy upholstery fabric on the sofabed and ottomans. Dark-brown modular wall units incorporate several white components to relieve the monotony of a total brown color scheme. A beige wall-to-wall carpet is punctuated by an area rug in a rich play of terra-cotta, brown, beige and blue. The rounded soft curves of the ottomans and the sofabed, which opens to become a round bed for sleeping, are repeated in the half-moon shape of the fireplace. All of these rounded soft curves, juxtaposed against the sharp angles of the wall unit and coffee table, create interest and visual excitement. So does the play of textures in the room. Aesthetically as well as functionally pleasing, the modular wall units contain a desk, a bar, a music system, and store books, clothes, china and linens.

With expansive but not expensive as her motto, designer Shirley Regendahl created this enchant-
ing one-room apartment. Money was saved on ephemeral things but spent wisely on a few good
basic pieces. A gay fabric used on the canopy bed and window wall dictates the overall color
scheme of pink, green, fuchsia and purple, which is repeated in various items throughout the
room. The brass canopied bed appears as a pagoda-topped sofa, with a pair of chests acting as a
dividing unit between the bed and the dining area. This consists of an expandable card table and
a pair of side chairs and provides intimate dining space, which can grow to service more than
two. The self-contained window treatment is a backdrop for this charming dining area, providing
both privacy and glare protection. At home in either the living room or bedroom portion of the
apartment, a comfortable pink upholstered chair further develops the color scheme. This is underscored by the lush plum shag rug which contrasts with the lime and orange appearing in the
kitchen area and the crisp lettuce of the louvered doors. All the accessories, dishes and placemats
were purchased from the five and dime. The substantial pieces of furniture were acquired one at
a time. With this clever stint and splurge technique it is possible to decorate on a budget, without
being shortchanged on quality.

101

decorating a one-room apartment, since decorating for one-room apartments can be so tricky.

A variety of pieces are available in see-through materials and metals today. These include all kinds of tables, desks, étagères, bookcases and shelving systems. Lucite and Plexiglas are also used in seating designs, such as chairs, loveseats and sofas.

Mirrored pieces are highly effective, for all of the same reasons. While not exactly see-through, these pieces have a reflective quality that is three-dimensional and so space-expanding by optical illusion.

• *Wall-Hung Furniture:* More than anywhere else, a one-room apartment needs wall-hung furniture. It is a fantastic space expander because it does not intrude on valuable floor area and provides for any number of needs.

There are many different units available today. These include shelves, cabinets, magazine racks and base storage cupboards. The latter provides surface space for television, stereo equipment and bar utensils. Many of these wall-hung combinations include a drop-leaf table that sees dual purpose as a desk and dining table, or a spot for sewing or tabletop hobbies and cards. A variety of systems are available in mahogany, teak, rosewood and natural oak, to name just a few. Styles vary, but mostly they are contemporary in feeling.

Most wall-hung furniture systems are a prudent buy for a one-room apartment. Apart from all their obvious functions of utilizing space to the fullest, they dismantle easily and can always be used in a larger home at a later date. The Danish systems are highly flexible when it comes to arranging the pieces on the wall panels, since items can be placed at will to create individual effects.

• *Modular Units:* Free-standing modular furniture is another space-saver in a studio or one-room apartment. This furniture comprises many different units, all of which can be used together to entirely furnish a room. There are units that fit against the wall and contain storage and display cabinets and shelves. Others have beds built in behind doors which are flush with the adjacent units. Some come with drop-down desks and tables, and some have display-storage cabinets that can act as room dividers, being of various heights, but not tall enough to block out light.

ACCESSORIES FOR INDIVIDUALITY

A one-room apartment that is on constant view needs lots of visual interest. One of the easiest ways to introduce this is through accessories. Accessories add that individual touch to your home, and highlight your personal interests and tastes.

Walls can be brightened with pictures and prints, or posters and inexpensive graphics if you are working on a limited budget. Mirrors, interesting ceramic plates, brackets holding ornaments, needlepoint or embroidered pictures all add to a plain wall and say something about you. Books can also add color and movement with their brightly illustrated jackets. Lamps are essential as a light source and they too can make a definitive statement about personal taste while adding decorative overtones.

A few decorative objects on tabletops create color-textural interest, but overdoing this will introduce a cluttered look, an easy trap to fall into with one-room living. So be selective with tabletop accessories and remember Mies van der Rohe's design philosophy: "Less is more."

Don't forget plants. They bring a touch of living greenery into the home and are a lovely accent to a one-room apartment. A tall plant contained in a handsome pot in one corner says more than an elaborate piece of furniture that takes up far too much space. A small indoor garden is easy to create and brings lots of visual interest to a room, especially when highlighted with a small floor spotlight at night.

6·HOW TO SHAPE LARGE SPACE

Large amounts of space can be just as difficult to decorate as small areas. Barnlike rooms and those designed on the open floor plan principle look marvelously spacious, but they often fail miserably because space has been badly planned and furniture poorly arranged.

The majority of these rooms do not live up to their potential because much of the space within the room is lost or wasted. In this instance, the design problem is controlling space effectively and shaping it intelligently, so that it functions in the best possible way.

The solutions for this kind of space problem are relatively simple, once you know and understand a few basic guidelines. The elements that are of vital importance are: 1. proper demarcation of space; 2. strong furniture arrangements; 3. visual definition through the use of various decorative elements, such as rugs, color schemes, furniture arrangements and, when necessary, room dividers.

The first step in shaping large space to your needs is to make a floor plan of the room. Explicit details for doing this are given on page 54, but very simply it is just a matter of measuring the room, translating the measurements from feet to inches, and drawing an outline of the room on graph paper. This outline is your blueprint for every stage of decorating the room, from planning the furniture arrangements to selecting color schemes.

When measuring the room it is wise to also measure existing furniture as well as any items you plan to buy later, so that you can make furniture templates to group on your floor plan (see page 36). In this way you will be able to ascertain just how much furniture you can include for comfort and convenience, and which will help the large space work best. Regroup furniture using the floor plan until you have the best arrangement for the room.

View the room from all angles. Walk around it to familiarize yourself with all its different aspects. Pay attention to the location of windows, any architectural elements or natural focal points such as a fireplace. All of these are of paramount importance in the formulation of your overall decorating plan.

This room seemed difficult to decorate at first, mainly because the living room opened directly onto the kitchen. Also, there seemed to be no logical spot to include furniture for dining. These problems were all overcome through clever decorating and skillful manipulation of large space. Key to the scheme is the L-shaped counter which was built around the kitchen area. It encloses the kitchen and separates it from the living room without creating visual blocks. The peninsula provides extra work surface for food preparation and doubles as a spot for dining, with the addition of tall wooden bar chairs. Ceiling-hung lights add extra visual definition. Once the peninsula was in position, the living room furniture arrangements fell into place automatically, including a dark-brown upholstered sofa and various other chairs placed around the room. Butcher-block tables echo the look of the counter. The brown-and-orange checked carpet pulls everything together, and because of its unbroken flow, expands space underfoot. The nylon carpet is ideal for this type of all-purpose room since it is hard-wearing and easy to maintain. Brick, wood, leather and other natural materials combine to create a relaxed ambience that is easy to live with, in a room where space has been thoughtfully planned.

105

In this living room of soaring dimensions Jane Victor works on the principle that important space needs important treatments. The designer selected furniture and art most suitable for the size of the room. She began her scheme by painting the walls a sunny yellow and the ceiling white. On the floor she used a large Moroccan rug in beige and browns, for pattern and textural play against the wood floor. In front of the fireplace she created an airy, open furniture grouping composed of a large sofa, coffee and end tables and two chairs. The sofa is upholstered in a brown-and-beige flame-stitch velvet, while the Plexiglas chairs have green velvet upholstery. An old cupboard was revamped through the addition of glass doors, which turned it into a display cabinet for accessories. An antique chest fills out the side wall and is balanced by the tall lamp and ceramic ornament. Clever placement of pictures adds further balance here, plus eye-catching visual interest. The crystal chandelier was chosen because its scale is right for the enormous room, and it also adds importance. Clever placement of furniture fills out this area of the room well, provides total comfort, yet promotes an airy ambience.

In this second view of the living room, the soaring window is visible. Jane Victor treated the window to white casements. The café curtains and tie-backs are light and airy and don't overpower the room. The wall facing the fireplace was covered with mirrored panels to create a feeling of more width in the somewhat narrow room. A brown velvet sofa and end tables form a second seating arrangement against the mirrored backdrop. The designer hung a large painting above the mirrored wall, almost at ceiling level, to reduce the barren look here.

MAKING SPACE GROW

This room analysis will help you to determine the right spots for major furniture groupings, as well as indicate where to create a focal point or center of interest, if one does not exist. Consider all the doors within the room and work out traffic patterns; these are just as important in a large room as in a small one. Be sure traffic patterns are natural and not contrived, and that they lead around rather than through major furniture arrangements, especially seating.

Incidentally, it is a mistake to think that a large room should automatically be filled with lots of furniture, simply to get rid of the barren look. Often this decorating technique will cause a crowded look, especially when the furniture is chosen haphazardly or is badly arranged. A large room will be much more attractive and functional when less furniture is used and arranged with skill.

DEMARCATE SPACE FIRST

When dealing with large amounts of space it is vital to plan your major seating arrangement first. Select the most suitable spot for it within the room. Once this major grouping has been properly positioned secondary seating will automatically fall into place.

• *The Living Room:* A large living room requires at least two good seating arrangements, possibly even three, if it is to live up to its potential. One seating arrangement that is large with lots of chairs and sofas will look spotty and unbalanced. It is not a good idea to centralize seating in this manner, because lots of upholstered furniture in one part of the room tends to create a heavy look, and it will then be difficult to pull together other pieces in the room cohesively. Then again, people do not always want to be crowded together in one conversation area.

The best place to position major seating pieces is around a natural focal point, if one exists, such as a fireplace or good windows. If you do not have a natural focal point, it is simple to create one, either with an interesting or dramatic piece of furniture, a large grouping of paintings or a special wall hanging. Alternatively, the major seating arrangement itself can become the focal point of the room, acting as the center of visual interest for the secondary seating arrangement and supplementary groupings of other furniture.

Once you have positioned the chief seating arrangement, select a spot for the secondary grouping. This can be just as large as the first, or smaller, depending on personal living needs and the actual dimensions of the room. It can be on an opposite wall, facing the major grouping; off to one side in the middle of the floor; or at one end of the room. But there should be some

108

A raised platform and built-in seating unit are the devices used to shape large space in this living room with a dining area. The room was divided into two separate areas through the addition of an L-shaped platform which runs along the back wall and down the side wall, in foreground of the picture. The back of the banquette was built on the raised platform, following the L shape, and with its protruding shelf adds further definition. Sheets from a new collection by Tai and Rosita Missoni are used throughout both areas of the room. The integrated designs in coordinated colors help to create a serene and personal ambience. The combinations of colors and patterns complement, harmonize and work together to achieve a fully coordinated decorating scheme. Some of the decorating ideas featured in the living and dining rooms include harem pillows on the banquette, folding screens, upholstered chair seats and ottoman, placemats and napkins—all done with sheets in stripes and florals. Additional sheeting is used on the back wall in individual panels to highlight this area. Cream walls and floor make a soft background. Room designed by Derek Mason.

Interior designer Leif Pedersen believes that large space looks and lives its best when several dominant pieces of furniture are used to make a strong statement. This was the basic decorating technique he adopted for a large bedroom and he produced striking good looks and total comfort. The focal point of the room is the grand bed with its ceiling-hung canopy, backdrop of matching fabric and tie-back curtains. For total coordination the designer utilized the same fabric for the sunburst-style lining inside the canopy, also for the upholstered headboard and quilted spread. The large French armoire perfectly balances the bed, and houses pull-out drawers for storing clothes and linen. The low chest at the foot of the bed, covered with linen and lacquered, provides additional storage and a spot for books and magazines. The tall étagère works as a serviceable and decorative night table, and again is harmonious with the scale of the bed and the armoire. A chaise and skirted table, in the foreground of the photograph, round out the room, where large space was brilliantly shaped to suit living needs.

110

separation between the two conversation areas, to provide for traffic patterns, and for basic good looks.

When grouping seating, don't forget to include end tables, coffee tables and lamps. They provide comfort and convenience and also a visual change of pace.

Once you have demarcated areas of space for your seating arrangements, you can plan the other supplementary groupings in the room. For instance, you may wish to include a desk and desk chair for a writing corner, or a game table with four chairs for cards and games. Many people create a library area at one end of the room, by including bookshelves, a chair and ottoman. If you are musically inclined, a piano may be an essential ingredient in your living room. Then again, a large living room may have to function for dining as well, and you must then select the most suitable spot in which to arrange dining furniture.

The main concern when decorating a very large room is to maintain a balanced and harmonious look. This is easy to achieve by pinpointing all the lost or wasted areas of space, after you have demarcated major groupings. Look for odd corners, short walls, blank walls between groupings, areas around the windows. These spots are perfect for a console, a small chest, a display cabinet or an étagère. If by adding any of these items you feel you will introduce that cluttered effect, then simply decorate the blank wall with a mirror, painting, or a large plant or collections of plants.

• *The Dining Room:* A large dining room is much easier to shape and control than a large living room. Obviously the dining table and chairs, plus a sideboard or server, are the most important pieces and will fall into place almost naturally. The middle of the room is the traditional place for the dining table, and a wall is the spot for the sideboard or server.

However, once you have allocated the space for these pieces, you may find you have a few blank spots in the room that need filling out to create a more furnished, well-balanced effect. For example, lost space can be treated to an étagère filled with decorative accessories and plants; a baker's rack, similarly treated; a console; a small chest or scaled-down sideboard utilized as a bar; or a wall-hung shelf for accessories and groupings of plants.

If your wasted area of space is small, dress it up with a painting or an eye-catching wall hanging. Another lovely idea is to put up wall shelves to display china, crystal or decorative objects.

• *The Master Bedroom:* In a bedroom, the bed (or beds) and night tables are your first consideration. They should be positioned on the most appropriate wall for comfort and convenience. You should then be able to organize the rest of the space for other furniture. First consider your needs. Expand the function of the room by adding a small desk or writing table with a chair; or

Space that was both enormous and unusual in shape was skillfully handled by designer Emy Leeser in this geodesic house. Built like a dome, with soaring ceilings and oddly angled walls, this interesting space was controlled by the designer through clever furniture groupings and use of color and texture. In the living room, walls are painted white and are balanced by rich texture and color underfoot. Tufted orange-and-yellow carpet runs wall to wall throughout the living room and into the entrance area. The major seating arrangement is positioned in the window area where a sloping yellow wall and lowered ceiling produce a more intimate feeling. A bright orange velvet sofa is teamed with four brown velvet armless chairs and a butcher-block coffee table; an area rug links and defines the area. Illumination is provided by the arc lamp which curves over into this part of the room. Ceiling-mounted spots supply overall light. A free-standing shelf–storage unit, left, visually divides the large space, also provides for accessories and books. The fireplace of black metal is balanced by the wall hanging.

Another view of this room shows a window alcove to the right of the furniture grouping just shown. The unique window creates dramatic impact all on its own, which designer Emy Leeser underscores with masks and a painting hung diagonally. Since the window is so dominant, the designer utilized a simple table and stools as the only furnishings in this area of the huge space. Plants add a touch of greenery and decorative interest.

113

In this same home, since the front door opens directly into the living room, Emy Leeser created the feeling of a separate entrance through some clever decorating. Most important element in the scheme is the circular area rug, patterned like a giant sunflower in vivid oranges and brown. Placed on top of the orange-yellow tufted carpet, it visually defines the entrance area, also focuses attention on the cantilevered staircase that swirls down from the higher floor. White pedestals, graduated in size, hold plants and sculpture and help to pinpoint this area as the hallway.

create a conversation area with a small loveseat and chairs; if there's enough space, add end tables and a coffee table. Be certain you leave plenty of free space for traffic patterns. These are just as important in a bedroom as in any other room. Blank spots in a bedroom can be treated in much the same manner as in living rooms and dining rooms. Add a single piece of attractive furniture, or decorate with accessories. Plants, too, can be used in a bedroom, to fill in an odd corner that looks lost.

HOW TO ARRANGE FURNITURE IN LARGE SPACE

In general, furniture should be arranged in airy, open groupings in a spacious room. If you follow this guideline at all times, you will add to the feeling of spaciousness and make the room look more balanced as a whole.

Avoid tight, overpacked groupings of furniture as these give the room a crowded look and create a sense of disharmony. Here are some basic tips which will help you control that large space for the best results:

1. Start any major grouping with the largest piece of furniture and make this the anchor of the grouping. Supplementary pieces will fall into place quite naturally.

2. Always separate very large pieces of furniture from each other—whether these are wood pieces or upholstered seating. When heavy or large items are too close to each other they create an imbalance resulting in isolated areas of space in the rest of the room which are difficult to decorate properly.

3. Arrange seating pieces in a flexible manner, so that the grouping can be enlarged or diminished to suit specific needs.

4. Provide for traffic patterns within the room. Be sure that traffic moves around and not through groupings, particularly seating and conversation areas.

5. Plan your lighting correctly, so that every area of the large room is comfortably illuminated and sets the right mood. Remember that a spacious area needs more light than a small one. It should also be evenly distributed for the best results.

6. Select furniture that is of the right scale for the large dimensions of the room. Several large-sized pieces are vital for true balance. Avoid very small pieces as they tend to look lost.

7. When choosing furniture, pay close attention to the scale and proportions of each piece to be sure they work well together. For example, don't partner a grand desk with a tiny desk chair, or a large sofa with a minute coffee table.

8. Plan your furniture arrangements so that they define space and suit

115

particular needs. They should have a self-contained look, while still being part of the overall room plan.

9. Consider using furniture groupings to actually divide a room, if necessary. A good grouping is most effective and will not create visual blocks or interfere with the flow of light and air. For example, a seating arrangement that is placed in the middle of the room, or protrudes into the center, will help to isolate one end and define it as the right spot in which to group dining furniture or create a desk-study corner.

10. When grouping furniture, don't forget the nearby walls. They should be treated to decorative paintings, wall hangings or mirrors. However, a word of warning: Don't hang wall accessories until you have positioned all of the furniture. Only then will you be able to create a balanced wall arrangement.

VISUAL EFFECTS THAT DEFINE AREAS

It is possible to define specific areas of space within a spacious room through the use of several visual effects. These underscore the definitions created by actual furniture arrangements and so help to promote a more finished look within the room. Let's take a look at some of these special visual effects.

• *Area Rugs:* Because an area rug introduces contrasts of color, pattern and texture to a floor, it can be used to define a specific area within a room.

For instance, a large area rug can be the anchor that pulls together and controls a furniture arrangement in the middle or at one end of the room. This "island" of color/texture/pattern immediately demarcates, since it isolates the specific furniture arrangement and gives it a self-contained look.

Two area rugs can be utilized in a large room to demarcate two distinct areas and create a feeling of separateness. When two rugs are used in one room it is wise to select styles that are either identical or well-matched with each other, for a sense of harmony.

In a room which contains three or four furniture arrangements, small area rugs can be used within the actual groupings to highlight each individual arrangement. This is a technique interior designer Angelo Donghia sometimes uses in a room which has a number of conversation areas. He utilizes small identical rugs. This idea is illustrated in one of his room designs in this chapter.

• *Color:* The use of different colors on the walls immediately defines one area from another visually. But color must be handled carefully. Select tones that blend well with each other for a sense of overall harmony.

Here are some ways to use color to create special visual effects and a feeling of definition in one room. Interior designer Joan Blutter lacquered one wall chocolate brown in an all-white room. All the seating pieces were arranged against the white walls, while the brown wall became a backdrop for steel-and-glass dining furniture, including the table, console-server and étagère, partnered with cane-and-chrome chairs. The brown wall introduced a feeling of separateness visually.

In a room where the basic color was yellow, interior designer Jane Victor painted one long wall bright kelly green. She then arranged a desk, chair and bookshelves against this green wall to define and demarcate the

This handsome room is actually the immense entrance hall in a modern house, and it was formerly wasted space until interior designer Leif Pedersen cleverly turned it into a comfortable second sitting room and bar with atrium overtones. To dispense with the somewhat barren and barnlike dimensions, the designer covered all of the entrance hall walls with wood paneling that adds richness and warmth as well as a feeling of greater intimacy. A large area rug introduces extra warmth along with pattern and textural interest underfoot; it also acts as the anchor for the major seating arrangement. This is composed of tan leather loveseats and chairs with chrome frames, a wood-and-chrome coffee table and chrome tubular occasional tables. Trees, plants and rocks were utilized by the designer on either side of the entrance hall and in front of the windows to introduce the atrium effect. The built-in bar was practically positioned to service two rooms opening off the second sitting room, as well as this central space. Since there are no doors on these rooms, a living room and a study, they are visible from the atrium–sitting room and vice versa. For this reason the designer skillfully blended colors, textures and patterns so that they coordinate from room to room, thus introducing real visual harmony and true cohesion.

work area from the rest of the living room. This same kelly green was repeated in a sofa at the far end of the room, against a yellow wall, for a feeling of color coordination within the room.

Interior designer John Elmo used bright blue lacquer paint on two walls of a room, to contrast effectively against a white-lacquered wall and the window wall treated to white full-length draperies. The designer then grouped two white sofas and blue-and-white plaid chairs against the two blue walls, and in so doing created a self-contained seating area. The white lacquered wall became a background for a desk and a free-standing bookshelf, along with a chair and ottoman for a den-study effect. Dining furniture was arranged in front of the white-draped windows. Here color was used to successfully define three separate areas within the one spacious room.

• *Dividers:* Dividers must be chosen carefully, because some tend to cut up a large room so badly that it loses its basic impact of spaciousness.

The best dividers to use are those that are light in scale, made of see-through materials or have open-work designs in wood or metal. None of these create real visual blocks, nor do they interfere with the flow of light or air.

Interior designer Leif Pedersen often uses étagères made of steel-and-glass to define areas within a large room, because they lend themselves to decorative treatments and don't stop the eye. He will sometimes place two étagères at the same point on opposite walls, jutting out into the room, to effectively separate a conversation grouping from a dining area or desk-work center.

This designer occasionally uses open-work carved wooden gates to create a sense of visual demarcation. He prefers the type which fold back to leave plenty of traffic space between and also to promote the feeling of uninterrupted space within the room.

A free-standing storage unit can be utilized as a room divider, providing the upper portion is composed of open shelves which do not block out areas of the room from each other. It is wise to select a lightly scaled piece, and preferably one with glass shelves.

It is important to shape and control large space so that it operates successfully for all your living needs. However, don't forget, the beauty of a large room is its very spaciousness, and this should never be diminished. To this end, always utilize furniture arrangements and visual effects that define and demarcate without breaking up the flow of space or counteracting the sense of airiness in the room.

The space in this large living room was carefully shaped so that it functions on two different levels. The room was divided in half through the simple addition of a large free-standing screen made of wood in an open-work design. It is set in the center of the floor, balanced on one side by plants; the other side is left free to permit access to the living room area. It visually demarcates specific areas yet does not block off one area of the room from the other. The black, brown and beige carpet made of hard-wearing polyester runs wall to wall and also helps to define the dining area. This is furnished with simple modern pieces that blend with the cream-coffee color scheme. The wine rack, native art objects and plants add decoratively without intruding on floor space.

119

MAKING SPACE GROW

The spacious feeling of this enormous living room is emphasized even more through clever decorating and skillful placement of furniture. To unify the many windows and create a smooth backdrop for the furniture, designer Leif Pedersen treated them all to one great sweep of floor-length draperies. Tied together by the angled valance, the white draperies cover three walls and help to expand the airy look created by white walls and the neutral color scheme based on white, beige, coffee and brown. Modular seating pieces of various shapes and heights form a unique conversation area at one end of the room, while French chairs and an ottoman make a secondary seating arrangement in front of the fireplace. The designer positioned the furniture to leave the central area open and free of clutter, for an extra feeling of space and for traffic patterns. The look is elegant, with the emphasis on comfort.

Interior designer Angelo Donghia wanted to expand the feeling of space in the large living room of his New York duplex. To this end he had the dark floor bleached to almost white and covered the ceiling with silver paper that reflects light, adds height. These treatments are balanced by dark fir-green walls that make a dramatic backdrop for the white upholstered furniture. To shape large space to suit his living needs, the designer created two major seating arrangements on opposite walls. Each one is composed of a large, plump, overstuffed sofa with lots of cushions, armless chairs and a good-sized coffee table. Ottomans and occasional tables are scattered around the room. Because the room is used for entertaining, furniture arrangements are flexible. Although sofas usually remain stationary against the walls, the various chairs are often moved to form other groupings as required. The designer believes this is an important facet when decorating large space. Seating should never be so "set" that it cannot be moved to cater to guests. Only other pieces in the room are a piano and bench, a large end table and a Coromandel screen. Trees and plants are used profusely. The room has comfort and elegance, and large space is properly controlled through good planning and careful placement of furniture.

121

7·CLEVER STORAGE IDEAS

Few families ever have enough storage space to meet all of their needs as things collect over the years. This is especially so in a growing family, where the demand for extra storage constantly increases.

In spite of the fact that storage space is of vital importance, most homes actually have inadequate amounts of storage that is often poorly located. And in many instances, the available space is badly planned and therefore not utilized as efficiently as it could be.

However, there are a variety of ways to overcome inadequate storage facilities and recover poorly used space. For instance, the existing space can be revamped to accommodate more things through careful planning and space-saving items.

When necessary, and space permitting, extra storage can be achieved through certain types of furniture, such as built-ins, wall-hung shelves, open-fronted cabinets, trunks, chests, cubes, storage walls and handsome straw and wicker baskets. All of the items just mentioned not only stow and stash, but introduce decorative overtones to the room as a whole.

Let's face it, a thousand and one things are needed to make a home run smoothly, but not all of them should be on view. Finding the right spot for them is imperative; most of them must be fairly readily accessible and within easy reach. This you can accomplish through a little ingenuity, imagination and reorganization.

HOW TO REORGANIZE EXISTING STORAGE SPACE

Even the tidiest people who run efficient homes are inclined to plan cupboards and closets poorly, so that the available space is inefficiently used. But cupboards, cabinets and closets can be totally revamped to hold twice as much as they already do. This may sound preposterous, but it is absolutely true.

The easiest way to begin is to simply take everything out of the particular closet or cabinet and sort the items into piles. Separate items used constantly from those used only occasionally. In this way you will ascertain the things which must be within easy reach, those items which can be stored on higher shelves or in the back of a closet.

● *Kitchen Cabinets and Cupboards:* It is something of a back-breaking job to reorganize kitchen cabinets, but it is worth it in the long run for the space you gain.

The only way to do it is to start from scratch. Remove every item from every cupboard or cabinet. Take all of these things into another room and spread them out, so that you can easily have the room to separate them into individual groups. Decide immediately which you can discard, either because they are too old, chipped, cracked or no longer needed. Be ruthless! We all have a habit of clinging to favorite things, but anything that is at all marred or useless should go. It is taking up valuable space.

Once you have sorted everything out, make a list of the types and number of kitchen organizers you require. Kitchen organizers include such things as plate racks, cup and saucer carrousels, single-, double- and triple-tier turntables—all of which help to expand cupboard and cabinet space because they permit you to stack and hang items. Made of plastic, they are relatively inexpensive and are available at all household stores and in most department stores. Don't forget broom and mop holders, vegetable racks, and cutlery organizers that fit neatly into drawers.

Once you have purchased these organizers, clean the cabinets and line them with shelf paper. Wash any items that are dusty before placing them back in the cabinets. Now you are ready to start reorganizing your cabinets.

Decide the most appropriate cabinets for the items. For example, the cupboard above the dishwasher is best for dishes used constantly; a cabinet near the stove is good for staples, spices and foodstuffs in everyday use. Better china and crystal should be placed in higher cabinets, as can any utensils used rarely. Drawers closest to the stove should house spoons, spatulas, ladles and forks. Pots and pans, casseroles, Dutch ovens, frying pans, bun tins and roasting pans should all be handy to a work surface and the oven if possible. Canned goods can be stacked in a higher cupboard or one in another area of the kitchen.

Utilize kitchen organizers in the most suitable cabinets for your general living needs. Make the most use of the inside of cabinet doors by adding caddies, pan lid racks and wrapping paper holders. Also, that cupboard

These photographs of my own long, narrow kitchen illustrate the ample number of cabinets above and below the sink–dishwasher area. Unfortunately, cupboard space always seemed to be inadequate mainly because of poor organization. A little clever planning, some reorganizing of china, crystal and staples, plus the utilization of kitchen cupboard and drawer organizers worked miracles. Cabinet space was stretched and a lot of wasted space was recovered. Cup and saucer carrousels, plate racks and flat turntables were used in the top and bottom cabinets. The same turntables, in single- and double-tier sizes, were also utilized to organize staples and other foods in the central cabinet. Cutlery trays were added to drawers, and I also took advantage of the backs of doors. This is wasted space that can be made to work overtime with the addition of the right kitchen organizers. All of these *items are inexpensive and available in household stores across the counter. Under the open cooking top, a cabinet was fitted with useful slide-out drawers for pots and pans; a lid rack was attached to the inside of the door. Copper and enameled-tin molds were hung in the space under the wall cabinets; apart from adding decorative touches, they free cabinet space.*

under the sink can be cleverly revamped to hold cleaning products neatly with a large turntable: tall items in the center, smaller containers on the outside for easy viewing. Mop and broom holders are simple to attach to the back and side walls of a broom closet, making room for other things. Look at the photographs of my own revamped kitchen closets in this chapter, for good ideas to adapt.

Cramped kitchen quarters need not cramp the cook in you, as proven in this big, bold treatment given this tiny Pullman designed by Edmund Motyka, A.S.I.D. The designer's theory-at-work is that in every chef's kitchen there is a place for everything and everything has its place, no matter what the space limitations are. Almost every gadget, dish, utensil, glass and linen in this miniscule kitchen may be readily reached, yet each is in a sense on display too. Shapes, textures and colors create pleasing order in what could otherwise be chaos. According to the designer, the decorative inspiration came from the new Art Nouveau-like vinyl floor covering that resembles leaded glass. It is sophisticated enough to take to the walls, and the designer utilized it on a portion of the back wall, for color/pattern interest and a feeling of continuity. The light and bright motif of the no-wax vinyl floor is repeated in the use of tinware, silver, pewter, stainless and glasses, which incidentally all add to the illusion of greater space. The adjoining broom closet was converted into a handy storage cupboard for crystal and wine. The door, covered in silver and white reflective wallpaper, meets another folding door to screen off this entire area from any other nearby activities. The designer added three roomy shelves along the back wall and these store and display all manner of essential items. Pegboard, taken floor to ceiling over the side wall, houses a variety of other utensils which can be hung on hooks.

Interior designer Edmund Motyka, A.S.I.D., gave this entrance in a country house total practicality and storage efficiency for coats, boots and other outdoor clothing, as well as skis. His technique was simple, and it can easily be adapted in any entrance. Four vertical dividers plus shelves were positioned along the back wall to apportion hanging and stacking space, as well as to demarcate end sections for the wall-mounted drums and for stacking skis. The back wall sections were painted white, emerald, yellow, red and blue, the same blue repeated for the trim on the verticals. With the simple addition of pegs, the central sections house coats and jackets. Fifteen metal drums were painted in the same vivid tones and then mounted to act as hold-alls for boots and other items. The metal blinds repeat all of the bright primary colors used for the storage wall; these tones balanced by the white brick floor, actually practical foam-backed sheet vinyl that stays clean and fresh, even in the worst weather.

128

• *Clothes Closets:* These too can be totally revamped to hold many more things, through better organization. Once again, the only way to begin is to remove everything and start from scratch. Sort clothing into groups, such as items worn constantly, occasionally or seasonally. Again, be ruthless and get rid of old, worn and outdated clothes, things you no longer like. It is always nice to donate these things to the Goodwill or Salvation Army. They are only taking up valuable storage space that could be better utilized.

Analyze the empty closet to ascertain whether you can add extra hanging rods or shelves or include sets of hangers that come attached to a wood strip that is fastened to the wall. The latter type of system is so well designed it enables you to provide three times the amount of hanging space in a standard-sized closet. If space permits add extra hanging rods, and shelves at ceiling level.

A variety of attractive closet accessories are available today that are not very expensive and do much to bring order to a closet.

Storage boxes can be utilized to hold out-of-season clothing. They easily stack on top of each other and can be placed on shelves in a closet.

Shoe bags and *shoe files* are designed to hang on walls; so make use of a closet wall or the inside of a door to organize shoes properly.

Handbag files that come attached to a hanger, with plastic compartments down each side, are very useful. Handbags simply slot into compartments and the file hangs in a closet next to clothes.

Metal shoe racks which are placed on the floor of a closet are inexpensive and do much to dispense with the clutter of shoes on the floor of a closet.

Tie racks which attach to the inside of a closet door or to a wall will efficiently organize ties, scarves and belts.

Plastic hanging bags are perfect for storing seasonal clothes and should be positioned at the back, if possible. Like storage boxes, they add a neat façade and keep clothes clean.

A lightweight chest can be used at the entrance of a closet, between the door and the hanging rods. Many of these are made of hardboard and are covered with fabric or quilted plastic in attractive colors. They provide lots of storage space, since drawers are of a good size, and hold shirts, sweaters, scarves, gloves and underwear.

FURNITURE THAT PROVIDES STORAGE

• *Cube Table:* The end table in the shape of a cube has become very popular because it can be used in many rooms and it offers built-in storage. Some

Consider this small living room where space was at a premium. Designer Virginia Frankel, A.S.I.D., used built-in banquettes along two walls, backed them up with shelf space behind, and finished off the arrangement with a large cube table that also functions as a bar. Both the banquettes and the giant cube conceal hidden storage space. The built-ins free most of the floor space, which is covered with polyester carpet in a soft champagne color. This, too, helps to stretch space underfoot. The essentially beige-brown room takes on the look of an Oriental bazaar through the use of Eastern accessories.

130

When the cushions are removed the lids of the seating banquettes lift up to reveal plenty of storage space for linens and other items. Cushions are made of foam rubber and covered in fake fur for total comfort. Similar banquettes can be used in dining rooms or bedrooms, are ideal for children's rooms.

Decorative bar and display center for plants and accessories is a hidden storage unit that holds major items, such as the bicycle shown, other sporting equipment, luggage, etc. Made of wood painted brown, it has a white plastic laminate top and the doors are decorated with panels of the same fabric used on the walls. Designed by Virginia Frankel, A.S.I.D.

cubes have lift-up top lids, others have concealed doors that work on the spring-latch system. Cubes are available in all sizes to suit individual needs. You can choose from a wide range of materials which includes natural woods, painted woods, plastic, and wood covered with plastic laminate or mirror.

A large-sized cube offers plenty of surface space for a lamp, plants and decorative accessories, plus a roomy interior for storage. Two smaller cubes on either side of a sofa work just as well and add a feeling of balance. Painted cubes or those covered with plastic laminate are ideal for children's rooms, since toys and other items can be stashed away out of sight. They also offer valuable tabletop space.

• *Trunk:* An old-fashioned metal trunk or one of the latest reproductions can be used as a coffee table in any room. They are highly decorative and at the same time give you plenty of interior space for storing linens, records, magazines and other items. Young interior designer Janet Shiff often uses a reproduction trunk as a coffee table, especially when she is decorating a one-room studio apartment. She prefers the style made of highly polished steel trimmed with brass on all the corners, because this is handsome and works with modern or traditional furnishings. When more surface space is required, Janet will add a large slab of heavy glass which protrudes several inches on all sides of the trunk. The glass top is simply removed when access to the trunk is required. She also likes to use a trunk at the foot of the bed in a master bedroom, and recommends them for children's rooms as well. She explains that most children love the idea of their own trunk, and when she is designing a room for two children, Janet gives each child his own trunk— often decorated with the child's initials in bright paint.

• *Shelves:* Open-fronted shelves can be used in any room of the home and in areas of wasted space, such as foyers, corridors and on landings. They are ideal as storage units because they make use of wall space and do not infringe on much-needed floor space. At the same time they can be highly decorative additions when treated to books, accessories, plants, attractive baskets and boxes. The latter can be ranged along the top or bottom shelves and utilized for storing items you don't want on view. Shelves also offer space for a television set, stereo equipment, records and tapes when used in a living room, bedroom or den. Open-fronted shelves can be a useful addition in a kitchen for storing china, glasses, copper utensils, cookbooks, staples and spices in pretty containers. In a child's room, shelves provide lots of space for books, plus toys and other possessions, and again they introduce decorative overtones to the room as a whole.

This spacious laundry is full of innovative ideas, not the least of which is the handy all-purpose storage cupboard, right. Open-fronted, it was built as a free-standing unit, so that it can be moved should the owners relocate. Space is included for ironing board, iron, washing products, vacuum, brooms and mop. There is even hanging space for clothes, a spot for the television and a convenient "dog house" for the pet. Designer Abbey Darer, A.S.I.D., makes total use of all the wall space through the inclusion of high and low cupboards. All manner of cleaning products and other household items are stored in the small cabinets at ceiling level, while larger base storage units next to the sink are used for sorting and storing dirty clothes. The drying board easily props into position and is ideal for sweaters and other items. It was covered with hardy indoor/outdoor carpet to match the floor. Three differently patterned vinyl wallcoverings are used throughout for decorative looks in this utility room; all are specially treated to withstand moisture and discoloration.

133

MAKING SPACE GROW

• *The Storage Wall:* Any wall in a room can be turned into a centralized area for storage. A storage wall can be created with wall-hung furniture systems, modular furniture or built-ins. Wall-hung furniture and modular units are prudent buys, since they can be moved into other rooms or other homes should you relocate. Of course the built-ins can also be moved, but you have the expense of ripping out and reinstalling them in the new home. Wall-hung furniture includes shelves, display cabinets with glass doors, storage cabinets of all sizes, to use high and low on the wall. Modular units are free-standing pieces which are placed against the wall, and like wall-hung furniture, they are made up of shelves, cabinets and cupboards.

If you prefer to create a storage wall with built-ins, make use of shelves as well as cupboards and cabinets for a change of pace. Shelves also permit you to introduce visual interest with books, accessories and plants. A wall of storage cabinets can be awfully dull to look at over a long period of time.

Although the storage wall is suitable for any room, it is particularly ideal for a children's room. Since it makes use of wall space, going up instead of out, floor space is liberated for games, playing, and other pieces of furniture. Yet at the same time toys and clutter are kept out of sight and are organized.

• *Baskets:* Decorative baskets of all shapes, sizes and designs have become very popular in the last few years. They are attractive additions in any room scheme and provide a place for storing all sorts of things. Baskets in various sizes can dress up a dull or empty corner in a room. Baskets can also be used on shelves, under desks and tables, within a storage wall arrangement or on top of cabinets. Some of the most unusual baskets are foreign imports, and it is worthwhile doing a little investigative shopping to find these items. Prices vary according to the style and size of the basket, but most are relatively inexpensive.

In this chapter there are lots of photographs which illustrate clever storage ideas from leading interior designers. All of them should inspire you to revamp your storage space efficiently, while introducing great good looks to enhance your home. Most of the ideas shown are simple to do yourself, and the majority are designed for limited budgets.

Wall-hung cabinets, shelves and baskets combine to provide lots of good-looking storage along this wall of a bedroom. As a matter of fact, all the furniture is on the wall except for the bed and the two chairs, freeing floor space as well as providing storage for every item. Interior designer Albert

134

Herbert, A.S.I.D., utilized two base cabinets with drawers, a wardrobe, plus
shelves and a dressing table unit to create the wallscape. The units are simply
hung on the rails attached to the wall through a unique mounting method of
pegs which fit directly into oblique holes. The shelves house books and
accessories, but could just as easily hold additional baskets for scarves and
sweaters. Baskets on the top of the unit store things not in frequent use. The
designer added a mirror with dressing-table lights to complete the arrangement. A similar arrangement could be created for a teenager's room, a children's room, or any other bedroom lacking storage facilities.

This honeycomb of practical storage space is created with panels joined together with ingenious black plastic connectors. These enable the system to be put together without any special tools or other hardware. Any arrangement can be created, building-block style, to suit individual storage needs. The wood panels are finished in scratchproof white lacquer and are available in three sizes. There is a base unit and colored sliding door panels as well, which can be used to build up other types of storage units. All the components are packed flat in easy-to-carry containers with instructions for the simple assembly. Here you can see how the panels have been formed into cubes to make a shelf unit plus a desk, through the addition of a large panel of wood painted to match. The cube units can be free-standing as shown, or placed against the wall. Since they are so hard-wearing, they are particularly suitable for children's rooms.

Here is an ingenious way to produce a full-fledged sewing space in the corner of almost any room. Interior designer Shirley Regendahl created this efficient and charming spot with a simple strutted framework, within which she hung fiber-glass-based window shades that act as decorative roll-down doors. Behind each, ample space has been allotted for every facet of sewing. The struts, in a handsome Dutch scarlet paint-color to match the tone of the floor, divide the built-in into four sections. The first is full-length to conceal a dress form and ironing board; the rest, with shelves, put everything within reach, including slide-in space for the portable sewing machine. Below the last three sections, more tuckaway space doubles as dresser drawers, when a guest stays over in this spare room. Wicker baskets, so popular today, provide additional storage on top of the installation, interspersed with greenery. This simple architectural ploy lends an air of lightness, as does a mirrored side—a very important accessory for dressmaking.

The shades over each section are made of fiber-glass yarns, are easy to install, and do not require the swing-out space of regular doors. They offer a smooth surface for do-it-yourself decoration, and wipe clean with a damp cloth. These fiber-glass shades hang straight, are fire- and fray-resistant as well. The amusing illustrations were adapted from The Golden Hands Complete Book of Dressmaking by the designer, and they make clever reference to the materials they conceal. The shade at the window is also set within a scarlet frame. As a final conversation piece, the shade-pulls were made from large spools covered with scarlet plastic to look like thread. At sewing time, the corner expands liberally for full duty. Afterward, working items vanish from sight behind the shades. This same idea can be used for storing other items in any room where space permits, and it is ideal for providing hanging space in a room without full-length closets.

Modular wall units can be used to provide more than adequate storage in any room, as illustrated here. This set of base cupboards and free-standing bookshelves help to create a neat and efficient home office at one end of a kitchen. Central storage cabinet opens to reveal filing cabinet, slide-out drawers plus typewriter shelf. Space underneath typewriter shelf houses telephone books and wastepaper basket. Cabinets on either side provide shelf and drawer space for all kitchen cooking utensils, china and linens.

8·RECOVERING WASTED SPACE

Surprising as it may seem, there is an enormous amount of wasted space in every home. Lost or dead space may exist in entrance foyers, corridors, landings, hallways, and in the rooms themselves. It could be wall or floor space that appears too small or too difficult to decorate.

Attics and basements are often neglected and so go to waste. Yet both these rooms can be revamped to function as comfortable living areas, through skillful decorating, a few ingenious ideas, and the use of the most appropriate products and furnishings.

Let's discuss these particular areas first, before focusing in on other lost space in the home, since both can add so much in livability, comfort and convenience.

ATTICS

That room under the eaves invariably goes to waste simply because most people are not sure how to decorate it effectively. Yet an attic has endless possibilities and can easily be turned into a second living room, a family room, a children's playroom, a hobby center, den or guest room, or a combination of these.

Three things are of importance in the revamping of an attic, if it is to live well. These are: insulation, soundproofing and lighting.

Some attics don't need insulation, of course, but others do, and when this is the case it's a good idea to talk to a local builder. A contractor will insulate the attic at a reasonable cost, although it's wise to get an estimate first. When money is a prime consideration, there are various insulating materials which are easy to handle yourself, such as a spray-on foam that hardens and fiber-glass wadding.

Once the insulating material is in place it can be disguised by a variety

139

Interior designers Douglas Sackfield and David Poisal designed this attic made into an attractive family room, which also becomes a guest room when required. The addition of glass panels in the pitched roof provides extra daylight. The sloping walls surrounding the new windows were painted a soft gold, all other walls were painted green while the ceiling was painted white. The feeling of spaciousness and height was thus increased. An extra-long 92″ sofa and a matching sofabed provide seating and sleeping facilities. Fabrics and finishes were selected with an eye toward easy maintenance. A collection of authentic eighteenth- and nineteenth-century Canadian furniture was used, for a highly individual look in a rejuvenated attic.

Here's how designer Shirley Regendahl carved a cozy haven out of difficult attic space. The inspired make-over began with new walls of plywood paneling and "built-out" window seats that help the deeply recessed windows hold their own decoratively against the heavily beamed ceiling. This basic space-lifting makes a perfect background for the charming, Shaker-inspired flavor of the furniture. The slanted roof is balanced by a roomy chest and, on either side, the windows become willing partners to the cosmetic touch-up. Ruffled valances and café curtains in brightly striped seersucker set off window shades in matching geranium. The bed is flanked by an end table–chest and a Shaker-like desk. Opposite the bed a pair of free-standing bookcases do double duty to provide TV viewing; while to one side, a pair of captain's chairs make a comfortable conversation area. A formerly wasted attic gets a revamp and becomes a charming bedroom high on style and comfort.

of wallcoverings, including fabric, wallpaper, wood paneling, planking and brightly colored decorative paneling. Which you select depends on your budget and personal taste.

When the attic walls and roof do not need insulation, you can treat them in the same way you would any other room in your home. Paint, lacquers, wallpaper, fabric and paneling are all ideal and introduce handsome decorative effects.

Soundproofing is vital in an attic, for the simple reason that it is at the top of a house and noise travels down. The simplest way to create soundproofing is to put down wall-to-wall carpeting or carpet tiles. Carpet is an excellent sound muffler, especially when used in combination with underlay or under-padding. Some carpeting comes with padding attached today; this is an economical buy and just as effective in diminishing noise.

For additional soundproofing, treat the walls to fabric, paneling, vinyl wallcoverings or cork tiles.

Good lighting is of prime consideration in any room and especially in an attic which often lacks adequate daylight. Before embarking on any costly remodeling, analyze the attic to ascertain whether artificial lighting will do the job properly. If not, get estimates from a local builder so that you know exactly how much new, larger windows are going to cost. If windows are not the answer, include lots of lighting fixtures and place them strategically for even distribution of light.

With these major elements taken care of, you can plan the decorative scheme of the attic. The furniture you utilize depends on the function of the attic, personal tastes and what you can afford to spend. But you can be less elaborate in this room, utilizing wicker, unfinished wood furniture painted bright colors, junk and thrift shop buys, even discards from other rooms in your home. A sofabed is always a wise buy for any attic, because it provides sleeping facilities for overnight guests when required. Good storage units are practical, especially bookshelves, cubes, trunks and baskets.

BASEMENTS

Almost any type of basement can be turned into comfortable living quarters today, mainly because of the new products now available that work well in this room.

There are several products which are suitable for use on basement floors. These are brick, rubber, asphalt tile, vinyl-asbestos tile and polypropylene olefine fiber carpet, sometimes called indoor/outdoor carpet. The one

Don't let a landing go to waste. Use it. Create a charming seating area within its precincts, as David Eugene Bell, A.S.I.D., has done in his client's duplex apartment. This is also an appropriate treatment for a country home. Use the staircase wall as a gallery for photographic portraits and give it extra impact. An antique Early American bench is snugly placed in a corner of the landing, with ample sofa pillows to cushion seating. An enlarged photograph is mounted and shown as you would display a priceless oil painting, and it's a good way to make a personal point in a home. Plants are clustered on the opposite side along with additional chairs. It is a lovely place to read, do some needlepoint, or have guests for afternoon tea. The hardwood floor is accented by the multicolored runners, and the period theme further enhanced by the one-of-a-kind clock.

you select depends on the effect you want to create and the amount of money you can afford to spend.

Treat the walls to several coats of paint or lacquer, unless of course you want to provide extra insulation with a heavy wallcovering. A wallcovering is a good idea when walls are badly marred.

Wood paneling, planking, plywood paneling in natural finishes, and plywood paneling with brightly colored finishes are certainly ideal for a basement. They hide a multitude of sins, add insulation and soundproofing qualities and produce handsome effects. Much of the plywood paneling available today, whether in natural wood or colored finishes, is relatively easy to install yourself. It comes in easy-to-handle panels, pre-cut to size, with total instructions for installation.

If you don't want to use paneling but wish to hide marred walls, you can utilize cork tiles, fabrics, and all manner of vinyl wallcoverings. They all introduce a smooth look to wall surfaces, but they are not as good insulators as paneling.

Proper illumination is imperative in a basement, especially so when this room is without windows. You should include plenty of well-distributed lighting fixtures.

Like an attic, a basement can be furnished with budget-wise furniture and castoffs from other rooms. However, all of these pieces should be dressed up with brightly colored lacquer, paint or wallcoverings, or alternatively refinished and polished to ensure good looks.

Depending on your specific living needs, a basement can be transformed into a recreation room, a children's playroom, a den, a home office, a hobby center, a family room or a comfortable spot for overnight guests. With a little clever decorating and careful choice of furniture, you can make it multipurpose, and it will then function for most of these requirements.

Convert wasted basement space to a multipurpose living area for the entire family by paneling walls and adding beams and lots of built-ins. Entered from the stairs behind the seating niche, the room's main remodeling material is paneling, chosen for its structural as well as decorative qualities. The handsome panels conceal stairs, cover bad basement walls and line the bookcase. The seating niche with overhead soffit for spotlighting eliminates the need for a sofa and lamps, also provides storage in the base. Ceiling beams were installed to add architectural interest to a conventional room, and are simple 2" x 3" lumber strips covered with leftover pieces of wood paneling. Furnishings and building materials are all easily maintained—from prefinished wallcovering to specially treated fabrics and plastic tables, as well as vinyl flooring. This practical family room gets lots of vitality from a cheerful red, yellow and blue color scheme.

ENTRANCES AND FOYERS

Entrances and foyers often represent wasted space in a home, whether this is an apartment or a house. Depending on its actual size, an entrance can be made to work overtime and serve for other living needs.

For instance, a good-sized foyer might easily become a home office with the simple addition of a desk or writing table and a chair. Alternatively, it can be transformed into a dining corner through the inclusion of a dining table and chairs of the proper scale. Through careful choice of furniture, an entrance can serve both purposes. For instance, a Parsons table or a steel-and-glass table can provide surface space for dining and paperwork.

If an entrance or foyer is too small for these particular treatments, analyze it carefully to see if there is any dead or lost wall space.

You will most likely find a wall that can be given open-fronted shelves or wall-hung furniture, to provide storage facilities and display space for accessories and plants. Certain other wall treatments can be utilized in a foyer, to make the best use of space and introduce decorative overtones at the same time.

For instance, you can add wall brackets to hold china ornaments or other objects in different materials, while wall-hung glass or metal shelves are perfect for housing an indoor garden of small plants. A wall can be given bookshelves to create a library ambience when filled with books, and when the shelves run floor to ceiling the effect is handsome.

Leif Pedersen transformed this dark corridor into a cheerful area through a couple of simple additions anyone can copy. A panel of floor-to-ceiling mirror adds to the illusion of extra light and space and is a "check-up" spot for guests. Since the corridor was too narrow for furniture, the designer utilized a wall-hung shelf for accessories and flowers, which adds a furnished look without intruding on the traffic lane. White ceramic tiles and geometric wallpaper flow through into the room at the end of the corridor for a feeling of greater space and airiness.

MAKING SPACE GROW

This hall yielded wall space for a small built-in vanity area which offers a spot for a last-minute grooming check. The treatment adds decoratively and recovers formerly wasted space. A lattice-print wallpaper covers a screen, which hides coat pegs in this no-closet foyer. The identical lattice print creates a backdrop for the vanity, which is actually a wall-hung drawer. Utilization of identical print in this way further enlarges the space. The drawer holds scarves, perfumes, combs, brushes and other items. A contemporary mirror matches the chrome-yellow used on the remaining portions of the wall. The umbrella stand adds a finishing touch. Designed by Emy Leeser.

LANDINGS AND SPACE BETWEEN ROOMS

A landing at the top of a staircase and space between rooms are the most common areas of dead space in some homes. This is because they are usually too small to decorate effectively. It is often possible to dress up this wall space with shelves, brackets, wall-hung furniture or small cabinets with glass fronts for displaying decorative objects.

Plants can also be cleverly utilized on landings and in dead space between rooms. A collection of plants in various sizes and of different species can be assembled to create a small indoor garden. They can either be grouped on the floor or stood on small tables, cubes or pedestals. When they are illuminated with a plant spotlight, placed on the floor, the effect can be most striking, especially at night.

When there is a reasonable amount of floor space available you can add one or two pieces of furniture to serve a specific need. For example, a small Parsons table and a simple chair create a home office; a selection of wall-hung furniture can provide storage-display space plus a writing corner.

A small area between a bedroom and bathroom can be furnished with an attractive table, stool and mirror to become a little vanity area for members of the family and guests alike.

A similar area of space between a kitchen and dining room can be transformed into a menu planning center, with the addition of wall-hung shelves for cookbooks and a drop-leaf shelf which works as a desk. A small bench or folding director's chair can be fitted neatly into such a corner to provide seating.

LOST WALL SPACE IN KITCHENS AND BATHS

- *Kitchens:* If you examine all the walls in your kitchen carefully you are sure to find areas which can be treated cleverly to become storage and display centers.
- Space between wall-hung cabinets and the countertop is an ideal spot to hang copper and tin molds. Use picture hooks hung at different levels to create an interesting look.
- Shelves can be added on all four walls of a kitchen at ceiling level, and they become decorative additions when attractive kitchenware is displayed on them. Utilize these shelves for large platters, propped against the wall, so that their patterns can be seen. Place large soup tureens and china casse-

It is possible to find lost space and make it function efficiently. This small area adjoining a bedroom was turned into an attractive little dressing room with the addition of a Plexiglas Parsons-style table and blue metal chair, plus a mirror and lamp. An olive carpet and bright blue accents pick up and sharpen the colors of the floral-striped vinyl wallcovering. The fabric-backed vinyl is easy to hang, and therefore a great do-it-yourself project. The wall-covering was installed both horizontally and vertically to further give the illusion of additional space, its change of pattern pace defined by the blue-painted chair rail. Any alcove such as this should be reconsidered and turned into useful space. Designed by Peggy Walker, A.S.I.D.

Use every inch of wall space in your kitchen to find a home for all your gourmet accessories and utensils. This cozy work area in a family kitchen makes cheerful, efficient use of butcher-block counters, modern ovenware, pegboard, shelving and old copper pots and pans. A work area and breakfast nook are created by using two butcher-block tables in an "L" arrangement. Pegboard is framed and mounted over work area and efficiently stores and displays all necessary cooking implements. Shelving over the breakfast nook, plus additional shelving around the perimeter of the kitchen and over the window frame holds additional utensils plus crockery and pots and pans. Hooks installed at strategic points display a functional collection of copper pots and pans. Wall-mounted light fixtures provide adequate lighting for cooking and eating. The gay, multicolored print of the carpet minimizes spots and stains, adds decoratively to the eat-in kitchen, also introduces a luxurious touch underfoot.

Odd bits of space have been put to use in this small old-fashioned bathroom remodeled by designer Edmund Motyka, A.S.I.D. He is responsible for the transformation through careful planning and clever selection of materials. Green-and-white patterned wall and floor coverings enhance the white cabinetry with a charcoal trim. The cabinets include a wall valet unit at the left, and a vanity around the sink with stack-on linen storage cabinets. All make the ultimate use of formerly wasted space, and the vanity hides formerly exposed pipes. Although a smaller sink was substituted, it is just as functional. A unifying effect is created by using a curved valance to enclose the curtained bathtub area, plus all remaining walls. Not one inch of space is wasted. Ample light is provided by the addition of a decorative fixture over the mirror. All surfaces, walls, furnishings and floor have washable characteristics, are simple to keep in pristine condition.

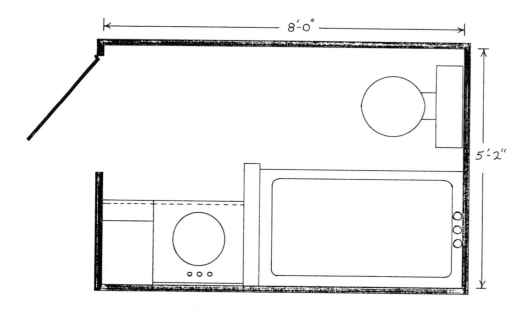

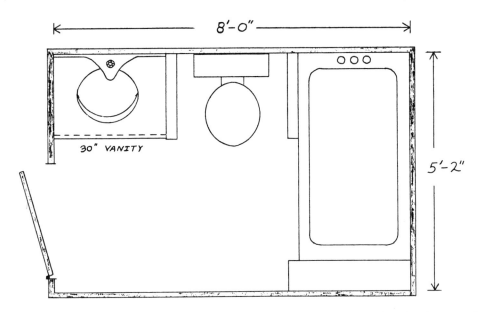

8'-0"

30" VANITY

5'-2"

One of the major problems in a bathroom is how to get rid of ugly pipes and at the same time obtain maximum use of space. A quick and easy solution is to add a vanity, thus hiding those unsightly plumbing horrors and gaining storage. In this bathroom, an elegant, classically designed 30" vanity is used. Exposed drawers provide ample storage for linen and miscellaneous items.

The marble top and the backsplash further accentuate a luxury look. Various sizes and finishes to fit the size and theme of your decorating scheme are available in cabinets and vanities. Swing-out doors provide easy access to the medicine cabinet. All elements have easy-maintenance qualities with no fuss or bother. This illustrates maximum use of space with the least clutter.

roles in front of the plates to utilize all the shelf space and promote extra visual interest. Attractive cooking ware that is seldom used can also be stored and displayed here. Use only one shelf along each wall, to avoid a top-heavy look.

• Wall space behind a stove or an open cooking top generally goes to waste. Recover it by adding a panel of pegboard, painted to coordinate with the overall kitchen color scheme. The pegboard becomes a handy catchall for a variety of utensils, small pots, molds, even a small rack for spices.

• If you own lots of good pots and pans and lack storage space for them, consider hanging them on the ceiling of the kitchen. They help to introduce a charming country mood, especially if they are of copper or enameled iron. Because most of these pans are usually rather heavy, be sure to use large hooks that are strong enough to take the weight.

• *Bathrooms:* Scrutinize your bathroom to pinpoint dead or lost space. You are bound to find areas on the walls which lend themselves to different treatments.

• That long stretch of wall over the tub is mostly a blind bit of wall, especially if it is partially tiled. However, you can treat the wall above the tiles to glass or metal shelves, running them almost the entire length of the wall if you wish. These shelves can be used to hold toiletries in attractive containers, plants, decorative objects and a perfumed candle.

• The short wall above the toilet may be just big enough to take a small shelf or a set of shelves for perfume bottles, a perfumed candle or plants, even a few paperback books. Sometimes you can fit a small cabinet into this meager wall space.

• Seek out odd bits of wall space, near the washbasin or bathtub, where you can add attractive brass or metal towel holders. They are not only practical but add a decorative touch.

• The inside of a bathroom door need not go to waste. If it is not utilized for hanging nightclothes, consider adding a mirrored cabinet. Today there are many new designs, slim and trim, for using on a door. They provide extra mirror facilities, as well as storage space, and since they are not bulky they do not interfere with the opening and closing of the door.

Recovering wasted space is not as difficult as it seems, once you know where to look for it in your home. And when it is treated practically and decoratively, you are making every inch of space earn its keep.

Peggy Walker, A.S.I.D., widened the horizons of a narrow galley kitchen by utilizing wall space. Ceiling-high shelves display and store all the spices and condiments needed, offer hanging room for various gadgets available to today's gourmet cook. Another new addition is a built-in countertop, which provides ample working space and in a pinch becomes an adequate breakfast nook. The walls were treated to a space-making pattern of small sunflowers and lush spring-green foliage on white vinyl, the floor to green carpet tiles. Everything is as practical as it is pretty, with easy upkeep. This is a great advantage in a kitchen where spills and cooking fumes are apt to settle. To one side of the window an old-fashioned iceman's tongs add a fun note, and beneath it an antique towel rack contributes another bit of old-fashioned spice and much-needed storage space.

CREDITS

PAGE

14 Collins & Aikman
16 Window Shade Manufacturers Association
17 Window Shade Manufacturers Association
18 U.S. Plywood/Division of Champion International
20 Jane Victor Associates
21 Emy Leeser/Photo Paulus Leeser
23 Window Shade Manufacturers Association
24 James Seeman Studios, Inc.
25 Imperial Wallcoverings
27 J. Josephson, Inc.
29 Window Shade Manufacturers Association
31 Burlington House Carpets/Burlington Industries, Inc.
32 J. P. Stevens Co., Inc.
33 J. P. Stevens Co., Inc.
37 Jane Victor Associates
38 Leif B. Pedersen, A.S.I.D./Photo Gleb Derujinsky
39 Leif B. Pedersen, A.S.I.D./Photo Gleb Derujinsky
40 Williams/Division Leigh Products, Inc.
41 Window Shade Manufacturers Association
45 Evans Products Company
46 Thayer Coggin, Inc.
47 Cado/Royal System, Inc.
48 Simmons Company
51 American Enka Company
52 Angelo Donghia, A.S.I.D./Interior Design Magazine/
      Photo Jaime Ardiles-Arce
53 Schoolfield Furniture Industries, Inc.
55 Cado/Royal System, Inc.
56 Simmons Company
57 Royal System, Inc.
59 James Seeman Studios, Inc.
60 American Enka Company
61 Bigelow-Sanford, Inc.
63 GAF Corporation
64 Jane Victor Associates
65 Window Shade Manufacturers Association
67 Tyndale, Inc.
69 Jane Victor Associates
71 Burlington House Carpets/Burlington Industries, Inc.
74 American Enka Company
75 Nina Lee, A.S.I.D./Photo Paulus Leeser
78 Bigelow-Sanford, Inc.
79 Window Shade Manufacturers Association
81 Allied Chemical Corporation
82 Armstrong Cork Company
83 Armstrong Cork Company
85 La Cour-Denno Associates, Inc./Photo Jaime Ardiles-
      Arce
86 La Cour-Denno Associates, Inc./Photo Jaime Ardiles-
      Arce

PAGE

87 La Cour-Denno Associates, Inc./Photo Jaime Ardiles-
      Arce
89–90 Jane Victor Associates
91 Schoolfield Furniture Industries, Inc.
92 Plywood Furniture Corp.
95 J. P. Stevens & Co., Inc.
97 La Cour-Denno Associates, Inc./Photo Jaime Ardiles-
      Arce
98 La Cour-Denno Associates, Inc./Photo Jaime Ardiles-
      Arce
100 Spherical Furniture
101 Window Shade Manufacturers Association
105 Du Pont Company
106 Jane Victor Associates
107 Jane Victor Associates
109 Fieldcrest
110 Leif B. Pedersen, A.S.I.D./Photo Gleb Derujinsky
112 Emy Leeser/Geodesic Structures, Inc./Photo Paulus
      Leeser
113 Emy Leeser/Geodesic Structures, Inc./Photo Paulus
      Leeser
114 Emy Leeser/Geodesic Structures, Inc./Photo Paulus
      Leeser
117 Leif B. Pedersen, A.S.I.D./Photo Gleb Derujinsky
119 Du Pont Company
120 Leif B. Pedersen, A.S.I.D./Photo Gleb Derujinsky
121 Angelo Donghia, A.S.I.D./Interior Design Magazine/
      Photo Jaime Ardiles-Arce
124 Rubbermaid, Inc.
125 Rubbermaid, Inc.
127 GAF Corporation
128 GAF Corporation
130 Eastman Chemical Products, Inc.
131 Eastman Chemical Products, Inc.
133 Magee Carpets/J. Josephson, Inc.
135 Royal System, Inc.
136 Cubex by Cado/Royal System, Inc.
137 Window Shade Manufacturers Association
138 Ethan Allen, Inc.
140 Simmons Company
141 Window Shade Manufacturers Assocation
143 Eastman Kodak Co.
145 U.S. Plywood/Division Champion International
147 Leif B. Pedersen, A.S.I.D./Photo Gleb Derujinsky
148 Emy Leeser
150 J. Josephson, Inc.
151 Du Pont Company
152 Williams Division/Leigh Products, Inc.
153 Williams Division/Leigh Products, Inc.
155 Window Shade Manufacturers Association

INDEX

accessories, 23, 34, 101, 102–3, 127, 143; large rooms, 106, 107, 111, 113, 114, 116, 117, 119, 121; *see also* specific rooms and areas

alcoves: dining areas, 63, 65; dressing room, 150; library, living room, 61; sleeping, 80, 81, 88–89, 90

asbestos tile, 88

attics, 139; children's room, 82, 83; furniture, 142; guest room, 140; hobby and family room, 71, 139; insulation, 139–42; lighting, 71, 142; soundproofing, 140

audio-visual equipment, 57, 58, 70, 86, 92, 96–99, 132

banquette: bedroom, 32, 33; children's room, 48; dining area, 67, 68; living room, 130–31; on platform in large room, 109

bar: in entrance hall, large, 117; in one-room (studio) apartment, 96–97, 99; as storage unit, 131

basement conversions, 142; family room, 24, 144–45; floors, 142–44; furniture, 144; lighting, 144–45; walls, 24, 144–45

baskets, 134, 137

bathroom, space-expanding techniques for: ceilings, 22, 40; doors, 154; fixtures, 40, 152–53; floor, 40, 152; lighting, 40, 152; storage, 40, 152; walls, 22, 24–25, 40, 152, 154; window, 40

bedrooms, large master, 110, 111–15

bedrooms, space-expanding techniques for: accessories, 52, 70; attic, 140–41; banquette, 32, 33; bed placement, 52, 53; bed treatments, 26, 32, 45, 52, 53; built-ins, 32, 33, 45, 48; carpets and rugs, 30, 52, 60; ceiling, 32, 52;

children's, *see* Children's rooms; dining area, 53; draperies, 30, 52, 60; dressing room, 150; floor, 32; furniture, 31, 32, 52, 53, 68, 69; lighting, 30, 69; living rooms as, 48; as office, 60; platform bed, 60; shutters, 32; as sitting room, 31, 52, 53, 60, 68–70; stereo and television equipment, 70; storage, 53, 132, 134–35; as study, 53; walls, 22, 31, 32, 45, 52, 53, 60; windows, 53, 69; *see also* Beds; Sleeping alcoves

beds, 70; bunk, 78, 79, 80; canopied, 69, 101, 110; one-room (studio) apartments, 90, 93; platform, 60; pull-down built-ins, 45, 58, 80, 87; sofas, divans, etc., 48, 56–57, 70, 71, 90, 93, 100; trundle, 80; *see also* Bedrooms; Children's rooms

blinds: slatted, 96–99; vertical, 14, 16, 41, 65

bookshelves, 24, 44, 47, 48, 60, 66, 132, 138; *see also* Storage, walls; specific room furniture

built-ins, 47–48; banquettes, 32–33, 48, 68, 130–31; beds, 45, 58, 80, 87; storage-display walls, 45, 47, 58, 134–35; *see also* specific room furniture

carpets and rugs, 13, 28, 34, 49, 150, 154; dual-purpose rooms and areas, 51, 55, 57, 58, 64; large areas and rooms, 105, 112–14, 116, 117, 119; manmade fibers, 32, 71, 88, 105; for platforms, 51, 60; soundproofing with, 142; as unifying element, 105; wallcovering, 71, 78; *see also* specific rooms

ceilings, 15, 22–23, 24; add-on architecture for dual-purpose

rooms, 59–60; mirrored, 22, 23, 66; painted, 71; soaring, in geodesic house, 112–13; *see also* specific rooms

ceramic tiles, floor, 13, 28

children's rooms, space-expanding techniques for, 73; alcoves, sleeping, 80, 81; attic room, 82, 83, 139–42; banquette, built-in, 48, 131; basement room, 144; beds, 75, 78–80, 83; bulletin board, 82; carpeting, 9, 74, 78, 81, 83; closet converted to sleeping area, 80; closets, 82; dividers for, 73–78, 79; draperies, 29, 74, 75; fabric coordination, 74, 77; floor, 28, 29; floor plan, and furniture arrangement, 73; guest facilities, 80; furniture, 29, 74, 75, 77–83; lighting, 78; nursery, 29; platform sleeping area, 80, 81; sitting room and play area, 75, 81; storage, 74, 78, 83, 132, 135, 136; wallpaper, 79; walls, 29, 74, 75, 78; window shelf, 82; windows, 29

closets: clothing, storage organization, 128, 129; conversion to child's sleeping area, 80; mirrored, 90

colors and color schemes, 13, 26–27; as dividers for room, 77, 118; large rooms, 116–18; monochromatic, 26, 31–33, 96; one-room (studio) apartments, 84, 91; related scheme, 96; window treatments, 42; *see also* specific room elements; subjects

copper wall panels and tiles, 13, 19, 25

cork tiles, 144

curtains, 53; beaded, 86; large rooms, 107

den, 70; attic room, 139–42; banquettes, built-in, 48; basement, 144; as guest room, 70–72; furniture, 70–72; -library, in living room, 59; -office, 38, 39; sewing and hobby room, 70–72

dining area, large rooms, 118, 199; counter, room-dividing, 105; platform, 109

dining area, space-expanding techniques for: accessories, 63, 65; alcoves, conversions of, 63, 65; banquette, built-in, 68; in bedroom, 53; buffet service, 62, 66, 67; fabric coordination, 61; floor, 66; floor covering, 65; floor plan, 37; in foyer, 88–89, 146; furniture, 16, 62, 63, 65, 68; furniture, dual-purpose, 55, 56, 57, 66, 68; in kitchen, 63, 65, 68, 105, 154; lighting, 16, 65; in living room, 51, 61–66; in one-room (studio) apartments, 86–88, 93, 94–95, 101; platform, 51, 65; space demarcation, 51, 62–63; walls, 63, 65; windows, 16, 51, 65; see also Dining room, space-expanding techniques for

dining room, large, 111

dining room, space-expanding techniques for: banquettes, built-in, 48, 67, 131; carpet, 25; ceiling, 66; draperies, 25; in foyer, 66–68; furniture, 25, 66–68; furniture, wall-hung, 68; in hallways and entrances, 66–68; mural, 25; -study, 35; walls, 22, 25, 66, 67; see also Dining area, space-expanding techniques for

dividers, for large areas, 118; counter, kitchen, 105; platform, 109; screen, 119

dividers, for small and medium rooms, 62; color as, 77; doors, louvered, 74, 76; furniture as, 62, 74, 76, 88–89, 91, 92, 96–97; panels, sliding, 77; pillars, 62–63; screens, 76, 90; shades, window, 76–77; wall, false, 73–76;

doors: French, window treatment for, 17; louvered, as room dividers, 74, 76

draperies, 15, 43; area-defining, 61, 63; colors, 42; fabrics, 42; floor-length, 44; for large rooms, 120; sheets as, 26, 94; see also specific rooms

dressing room, 150

dual-purpose rooms, see Room within a room; desired uses

entertainment area, casual: in bedroom, 52, 53, 60; dining area, kitchen, 63

entrance hall: dining room in, 67; large, as sitting room, 117; see also Foyers and entries, and space expansion; Halls

entries, see Foyers and entries, and space expansion

fabrics, 15; cabinet door decoration, 131; coordination, in dual-purpose room, 61; drapery (see also Draperies), 42; patterns, 15, 49, 91, 94–95; sheets, use of, 26, 32, 94–95, 109; upholstery, 26, 30; wall coverings, 19, 26, 61, 131, 144

family room: attic, 139–42; basement, 24, 144–45;

floors and floor coverings for large rooms, 105, 112–13; carpets and rugs, 105, 112–14, 116, 117, 119; platform, 109

floors, floor coverings, and space expansion, 13, 27–28, 31, 49; asbestos tile, 88; carpeted, see Carpets and rugs; ceramic tile, 13, 28; dual-purpose rooms and areas, 51, 55, 57, 58; floor plans and furniture arrangements, 35–36, 37, 54, 73, 104; linoleum, 28, 88; marble, 13, 28, 66; painted floors, 13, 28, 49, 86, 88; patterned, 28, 84–88; platforms, 51, 60, 65; rugs, see Carpets and rugs; space demarcation, 58, 77; stencil designs, 28; vinyl sheets and tiles, 13, 23, 28, 49, 65, 66, 88, 128; wood, bleached, 49; wood, natural, 13, 28, 29, 49, 88; see also specific rooms

foyers and entries, and space expansion, 146; accessories, 27, 146, 148; ceiling, 27; dining area, 88–89, 146; dining rooms in, 66–68; dining room-study, 55; floor, 27; office, 146; storage, 27, 128, 146; vanity area, 67, 148; walls, 146–48

furniture, for large rooms: arrangements, tips for, 115–16; bedroom, 110, 111–15; dining room, 111; floor plans, and arrangement of, 104; living rooms, 105–13, 120–21; as room divider, 118

furniture, space-expanding, 13, 14, 16, 17; alternatives to furniture, 14; arranging, tips for, 36–41; audio-visual equipment, 57, 58, 70, 86, 92, 96–99, 132; baskets, 134, 135, 137;

built-ins, 45, 47–48, 80, 87, 130–31, 134; as dividers for room, 62, 74, 76, 88–89, 91, 92, 96–97; dual-purpose, 44, 54–58, 66; floor plans, and arrangement of, 35–36, 37; mirrored, 102; modular, free-standing, 45, 58, 102; modular seating, 45–47, 48; painted, 13, 30; plastic-laminated, 91, 131; scale, 30, 36; see-through, 13, 19, 30, 40, 62, 82, 99–102; as storage space, 129–136; trunks, 132; upholstery fabrics, 26, 30, 40; upholstery, mylar, 96–97; wall-hung, 44, 47, 57, 102, 134–35; and wall treatment, 19, 20, 22, 49; wicker and bamboo, 30, 63; see also specific rooms

guest facilities; attic rooms, 139–42; basement room, 144; children's room, 80; den, 70–72; in one-room (studio) apartment, 87, 96–97

glass and glass combinations, see Furniture, see-through; specific room furniture

halls: dining room in, 67; landings, 143, 149; large, as sitting room, 117; walls and ceilings, mirrored, 22, 23; see also Foyers and entries, and space expansion

hobby room: attic, 139–42; basement, 144; den as, 70–72; sewing corner, 137

illusion, visual, 13–34

kitchen, and living room area, 105

kitchens, space-expanding techniques for: carpet, 151, 154; ceiling, 23; counters, 151, 155; dining areas, 63, 65, 68, 105, 154; floor, 23; galley, 155; lighting, 105, 151; menu-planning center, 149; office, 138; storage space and organization, 23, 122–27, 132, 138, 149–54, 155; wall covering, 65, 155; walls, 23, 24–25, 149–54, 155; windows, 23, 65

lambrequin, 44

landings, 149; seating area on, 143

large rooms, 104; area definition, visual, 116–18; carpets and rugs, 105, 112–14, 116, 117, 119; color schemes, 116–18; dividers for, 118, 119; emphasizing size of, 120–21; familiarizing yourself with, 104, 108; floor plans, and furniture arrangement, 104; kitchen, in living room area, 105; lighting, 106, 115; space demarcation, 109–15; see also specific rooms

laundry room, 133

library: alcove, 63; -den, in living room, 59, 66

lighting: attic room, 71, 142; basement room, 144–45; kitchen, 105, 151; for large rooms, 106, 115; sunlight simulation, 39; and walls, 22

linoleum, 28, 88

living room, large: accessories and plants, 106, 107, 111, 113, 114; banquette, 109; carpets and rugs, 105, 112–14; dining areas, 105, 109, 111, 118, 119; draperies, 120; emphasizing size of, 120–21; entrance area, 114; furniture, 105–113, 120–21; and kitchen area, 105; lighting, 106; platform, 109; walls, 106, 109, 111, 112–13, 120–21; windows, 107, 111, 113

living rooms, space-expanding techniques for: accessories and plants, 14, 57, 64, 130; built-ins, for storage, 130–31; carpets and rugs, 14, 20, 21, 47, 64; as bedroom, 48; ceiling, 17; dining, alcove, conversions of, 63, 65; dining area, 51, 61–66; draperies, 14, 64; fabric coordination, 61; floor, bare, 46; floor plan, typical, 37; furniture, 14, 17, 20, 21, 41, 47; furniture, dual-purpose, 48, 56–58; furniture, modular, 46–47, 48; furniture, wall-hung, 47, 64; game area, 64; library, alcove, 63; library-den, 59, 66; lighting, 64; murals, 14, 21; office, 57; pillows, 40; shelf slab, 14; storage, 47, 130–32; walls, 14, 17, 18, 20–22, 46; windows, 17, 41, 46, 61, 64; see also main subject entries (furniture, etc.)

louvers, 44

lucite, see Furniture, see-through; specific room furniture

medium-sized room, 14; floor plan, typical, 37; see also specific rooms, subjects

metal panels and tiles, 13, 19, 25

metallic wall coverings, 13, 22–25

mirrors: ceiling, 22, 23, 66; on furniture, 102; on screens, 90; as table settings, 16

mirrors, wall, 13, 16, 19–22, 23, 24, 66, 67; black, 49; in closets, 90; and furniture, 19–22, 49; for large room, 107; and lighting, 22

murals, 25–26, 59; graphics, 13, 21, 26, 86; trompe l'oeil, 13, 24, 25–26

narrow rooms, 17

nursery, 29

office: basement room, 144; bedroom, 60; den, 38, 39; dining room, 55; in foyer, 146; in kitchen, 138; on landing, 149; living room, 57; furniture, dual-purpose, 55, 56, 57

one-room (studio) apartments, 84; accessories, 101, 102–3; budget-conscious decorating, 101; carpets and rugs, 88, 90, 91, 94–95, 100, 101; closets, 87; color schemes, 84, 86, 91, 94–99; dining area, 86–88, 93, 94–95, 101; dividing the room, 88–89, 91, 92, 96–97; draperies, 94; entertaining facilities, 96–97, 98; floor coverings, 84–88; floor plan, and furniture arrangement, 88; furniture, 87–102; furniture arrangement, flexibility of, 94; guest facilities, 87, 96–97; lighting, 88, 98–99, 103; pattern use, 84–88, 91, 94–95; shape, use of, 100; sheets, decorating with, 94–95; sleeping arrangements, 87–90, 92, 94–95; stereo and television equipment, 86, 92, 96–99; storage, 87, 88, 91, 93–94, 100; walls, 87, 88, 90, 96–99; windows, 86, 88, 90, 92, 96–97

paneling, wall, 63, 144–45

panels, sliding: as room dividers, 77; for window, 14, 43

patterns, 34, 42, 49; fabrics, 15, 49, 91, 94–95; floor coverings, 28, 84–88; wall coverings (see also Murals), 13, 17, 34, 42, 49, 59, 148

pillars, floor to ceiling, as room dividers, 62–63

planning, 35, 104, 108; floor plans and furniture arrangement, 35–36, 37, 54, 73, 104; taste, personal, 19

plants, 23, 103; for landings, 143, 148; as room dividers, 62; spotlighting, 103, 149; see also Accessories; specific room accessories

platforms: bed, 60, 80, 81; dining area, 51, 65; dining area, large room, 109

Plexiglas, see Furniture, see-through materials; specific room furniture

porch, converted, 17

room within a room, 50–53; dividers, 62–63; floor plan, 54; floor treatments, 58, 62; furniture, dual-purpose, 54–58; platforms, 51, 60; wall treatments, 58–60; see also uses

rugs, see Carpets and rugs

screens, 109; mirrored, 90; room-dividing, 62, 119; shoji, 14, 43, 88–89

sewing area: corner, 137; den as, 70–72

shades, bamboo, 18

shades, window, 15, 29, 42–43, 65; for French doors, 17; as room dividers, 76–77, 79; as storage-cabinet doors, 137

sheets, decorating with, 26, 32, 94–95, 109

shelves, 66, 132; see-through, 17; slabs, wall, 14; wall-hung, 55, 57; see also Bookshelves; storage, walls

shoji screens, 15, 43, 88–89

shutters, 14, 43

sitting room: bedroom as, 31, 52, 53, 60, 68–70; children's room, 75, 81; entrance hall, large, as, 117; see also Living rooms, space-expanding techniques for

sleeping alcoves: children's rooms 80, 81; one-room (studio) apartments, 88–89, 90; see also Bedrooms

sliding panels: as room dividers, 77; for window, 14, 43

soundproofing, 142

stereo systems, 57, 58, 70, 86, 92, 96–99, 132

storage, 122; banquettes, 130–31; bins, 83; bar and display center, 131; baskets, 134, 135, 137; clothing, 128, 129; cube tables, 129–32; cube units, 136; drums, 128; entrance area, 128; reorganizing existing space, 122–123; room dividers, 118; shelves, 132; trunks, 132; walls, 44, 134–35; see also specific rooms and areas and their furniture

studios, see One-room (studio) apartments

study: bedroom as, 53; corner, 93; and dining room, 55

MAKING SPACE GROW

swags and valance, 42; *see also* Draperies

taste, personal, 19
television sets, 57, 58, 70, 86, 92, 96–99, 132
textures, 14, 59
tiles, *see* specific materials (ceramic, vinyl, etc.)
trunks, 132

utility room, 133

vanity area: between rooms, 149; in foyer, 63, 148
vinyl: flooring, sheets and tiles, 13, 23, 28, 49, 65, 66, 88, 128; wall coverings, 133, 142, 144, 150, 155

wall coverings, 13, 15–19; carpet, 71, 78; cork tiles, 144; fabric, 19, 21, 26, 131, 144; metal sheets and tiles, 13, 19, 22–25; metallic, 13, 22–25; patterned (*see also* Murals), 13, 17, 34, 42, 49, 59, 148; space demarcation, 58–59; vinyl, 133, 142, 144, 150; wallpaper (*see also* Murals), 19; *see also* Walls; specific room walls
wallpaper, 19; murals, 13, 21, 24, 25–26, 59, 86
walls, of large rooms, 106, 107, 109, 111–13, 118, 120, 121
walls, space expansion and, 13–21, 31; accessories, 103; add-on architecture, 59–60, 67; and ceilings, 15, 16, 22–23; dual-purpose rooms, 58–60; false, 18, 51, 73–76, 81; furniture hung on, 44, 47, 57, 102, 134–35; mirrored, *see* Mirrors, wall; painted, 19, 24, 26–27, 49, 59, 71; paneled, 63, 144–45;

plywood strips on, 60; shelf slabs, 14; shelves hung on, 55, 57; soundproofing, 142; space demarcation, 58–60; storage-display, 45, 47, 58, 134–35; *see also* Wall coverings; specific rooms
wasted space, recovering: attics, 71, 82–83, 139–42; basements, 24, 142–145; bathrooms, 152–53, 154; between rooms, 148; entrances and foyers, 146–48; landings, 143, 149; kitchens, 149–54
windows, 42–44; attic rooms, 71, 140, 141; bay, 61; blinds, 14, 16, 41, 65, 96–99; curtained, 53, 86, 107; draperies, *see* Draperies; false, 39; lambrequin, 44; large rooms, 107, 111, 113; picture, in kitchen, 65; shades, 15, 29, 42–43, 65; shoji screens, 15, 43, 88–89; sliding, for panels, 14, 43; stained-glass, 92; walls to camouflage, 51; *see also* specific rooms

160